Have You Ever Had a Boss That …

Have You Ever Had a Boss That …

Succeeding in a Dysfunctional Workplace

Eric Charran

BUSINESS EXPERT PRESS
Leader in applied, concise business books

Have You Ever Had a Boss That: Succeeding in a Dysfunctional Workplace

First published in 2025 by
Business Expert Press, LLC
222 East 46th Street, New York, NY 10017
www.businessexpertpress.com

ISBN-13: 978-1-63742-770-5 (paperback)
ISBN-13: 978-1-63742-771-2 (e-book)

Business Expert Press Business Career Development Collection

First edition: 2025

10 9 8 7 6 5 4 3 2 1

To my wife Stephanie and my kids Carter, Serena, and Sylvia, my family and friends, for their endless support and encouragement.

To all pioneers, whether bold or timid and all in-between, you are all valuable stars

Description

In today's corporate landscape, professionals at every level—from early career to senior executives—face the challenge of working with difficult managers.

Have You Ever Had a Boss That... Succeeding in a Dysfunctional Workplace provides **actionable strategies** to help you not only cope but also excel in even the most dysfunctional environments. Drawing from extensive research and real-life experiences, this book explores different types of difficult managers and offers tailored advice for thriving at every career stage.

Whether you're just starting out, managing a team, or leading an organization, this essential guide will equip you with the tools to navigate workplace challenges and build lasting success.

Contents

Preface

The inspiration for this book was born from my own trials, tribulations, and learnings throughout my professional journey. As I navigated the complexities of working with difficult managers and challenging workplace dynamics, I often found myself wishing for a guide—a resource that could offer practical advice and emotional support. My hope is that by sharing my experiences and the strategies I've developed, this book will make your professional life easier and more impactful, leading to greater satisfaction and success.

Reflecting on my career and authoring this book was a journey in itself. I had a lot more fun than I expected recalling, recounting, and crafting the managerial and leadership archetypes. These archetypes are drawn from real-life experiences, and I hope you'll enjoy reading about them as much as I enjoyed writing about them. Whether you find yourself commiserating with the scenarios or identifying with the archetypes, I believe you'll discover valuable insights and have a few laughs along the way.

Had I written this book earlier in my career, it would have been a vastly different work. In those days, my approach to dealing with difficult managers was more mercurial and tactical, focused on immediate problem-solving rather than long-term relationship-building. Over time, I learned the immense value of emotional intelligence and empathy—skills that, admittedly, I honed later in life than most. These qualities are the cornerstones of effective leadership and management, and they have transformed the way I navigate professional challenges.

I often tell my son to be more like Superman than Lex Luthor. Superman, with all his incredible abilities, chooses to use his powers for the greater good, bringing humanity along on his journey. In contrast, Lex Luthor, despite his brilliance, is primarily focused on advancing himself, often at the expense of others. This analogy underscores a fundamental principle I hope to convey in this book: true leadership and professional success come from empathy, collaboration, and a commitment to helping others thrive.

As you delve into the pages of this book, I encourage you to reflect on your own experiences and consider how the strategies and insights shared here can be applied to your unique situation. The journey to professional satisfaction and success is seldom straightforward, but with the right tools and mindset, it can be immensely rewarding. Thank you for joining me on this journey. I hope that *Have You Ever Had a Boss That ...* will serve as a valuable companion and guide in your professional life.

Introduction

Stepping into the vibrant and fast-paced world of my early career, I was immediately struck by the influence and aura of leaders across various sectors, not just in IT and technology. Managers, with their diverse titles and roles, universally symbolized a wealth of experience and success. They seemed to naturally embody the qualifications necessary for steering not just projects but the careers of those they led. Regardless of industry—be it health care, finance, or technology—these figures represented the pinnacle of professional achievement.

As a young professional, my interactions with these leaders were colored by both respect and ambition. I often found myself pondering, "What paths did they take to reach these heights? What decisions propelled them into these roles of influence? And crucially, what steps could I take to emulate their success?" These weren't just passing curiosities, but intense questions driven by a desire to navigate my own career trajectory effectively.

In each meeting, email exchange, or project review, I saw these leaders not just as supervisors but as gateways to potential opportunities for advancement—promotions, skill enhancements, and pivotal assignments. This is a common sentiment, one likely shared by many of you, who recognize the crucial role these leaders play in our professional lives. Yet, as I progressed and took on more responsibilities, the initial sheen of infallibility that I attributed to my managers began to tarnish. I encountered decisions that baffled me, strategies that seemed short-sighted, and leadership styles that varied wildly from one person to another.

This book dives deep into the heart of these interactions, offering more than just a reflection on varied managerial styles. It aims to arm you with strategies to effectively engage with and adapt to these styles, enhancing your ability to work under any type of leadership. Through relatable anecdotes and actionable advice, the goal is to transform your understanding of these dynamics from potential sources of workplace stress to opportunities for profound personal growth and career advancement.

Understanding that these challenges are not indicative of "bad bosses" but rather complex behaviors that can be navigated and mastered, this book does not criticize but enlightens. It seeks to equip you with the knowledge to recognize, understand, and optimize your interactions with all types of managers. By doing so, you will be empowered to not only survive but also thrive in today's ever-evolving professional environments, making each managerial relationship a steppingstone to greater success.

So, whether you're just starting out or are well into your career journey, this book endeavors to be an invaluable companion, providing insights that will help you navigate the complexities of working with diverse leadership styles. Here, you'll learn not just to cope, but to excel, turning everyday challenges into your most rewarding opportunities.

What to Expect

Throughout this book, we meticulously categorize key managerial behaviors into distinctive archetypes, providing you with a structured lens to navigate the complexities of various—and often challenging—managerial styles. This approach will enable you to identify specific traits and behaviors in your leaders, fostering a deeper understanding of actions that may initially appear perplexing or frustrating. As you explore each chapter, you may recognize these behaviors from your own professional encounters. Every archetype, from the enigmatic The Surprised to the reactive LIFO manager, comes to life through vivid descriptions and real-world examples, presented in a clear narrative style. This exploration helps you not only recognize different behaviors but also understand the underlying motivations—whether it's due to your boss being overstretched, wrestling with skill deficits, or dealing with gaps in professional maturity.

For each archetype discussed, we delve deep into the reasons and causes behind the behaviors exhibited. This insight is crucial for developing emotional intelligence and empathy, allowing you to employ effective strategic coping techniques. By understanding the "why" behind the behaviors, you enhance your ability to manage interactions and even assist in the development of your manager, potentially mitigating problematic behaviors. This analytical approach bridges the gap between merely identifying managerial archetypes and understanding their practical implications on team dynamics, morale, productivity, and success.

We conclude each archetype discussion with a comprehensive toolkit of strategies, enriched by "Putting it Into Practice" sections. These segments, filled with narrative-driven conversational examples, demonstrate how to implement these strategies amidst anticipated resistance to change. Whether you're learning to preempt the needs of "The Amnesiac Manager," inspiring a "Firefighter Manager" to adopt a more strategic approach or navigating the complexities of the "Order Taker" manager, these strategies are designed to provide immediate value and empower you to take charge of your professional interactions. By the end of the book, you'll not only have a thorough understanding of various managerial archetypes but also practical tools at your disposal. This book sets the stage for a journey of personal and professional growth, preparing you to meet and manage the challenges posed by diverse leadership styles with confidence and expertise.

Strap in and get your highlighters ready—we're about to turn insights into actionable breakthroughs in this adventurous deep dive into the world of managerial quirks and how to handle them like a pro.

PART 1

Foundational Managerial Archetypes

CHAPTER 1

The Surprised

Background

Anil, a Vice President of Analytics at a leading financial services organization, had carved a niche for himself as a deep technologist with a sharp acumen for analytical techniques, platforms, and architectures. Originating from an engineering director role, Anil had honed his skills in a world where data spoke louder than words, leading a compact team with precision and a keen oversight that allowed for an intimate knowledge of each member's contributions. This microcosm of productivity and innovation was Anil's domain, a realm where challenges were met with swift, tech-driven solutions, and leadership was about steering a tight-knit crew through the complex seas of data analysis.

The departure of Senior Vice President Rina marked a turning point in Anil's career. Elevated from his role to fill the vacuum left by Rina, Anil transitioned from a provisional leader serving in the interim to an official position at the helm of a thousand-strong organization. This new role was worlds apart from the familiar territory of leading a small team. Suddenly, Anil found himself at the apex of a vast hierarchy, a sprawling network of teams and subteams whose individual activities became an enigma.

Inheriting a cadre of capable vice presidents (his former peers), Anil grappled with the organizational depth, struggling to grasp the myriad functions and operations that now fell under his purview. Leadership calls, once an arena of confidence and command, morphed into sessions of revelation and surprise. Unacquainted with the granularities of his expanded domain, Anil frequently encountered problems, issues, and challenges that seemed to emerge from the ether, leaving him feeling adrift in a sea of unknowns.

The discomfort of being out of touch with the organization's pulse manifested in public admonishments. When vice presidents brought issues to light during leadership discussions—issues that were news to Anil—his response was often one of visible frustration and disbelief. "How is this the first time I'm hearing about this?" became a refrain that echoed through the ranks, a symbol of Anil's struggle to transition from the world of direct control to the vast expanse of strategic leadership. This scenario not only highlighted the challenges inherent in scaling personal management styles to larger teams but also underscored the critical need for effective communication and understanding within the multilayered structure of a leading organization.

In a meeting with William, the Chief Information Officer (CIO), Anil and his team of vice presidents were delivering the results of their latest quarterly business review. As the teams transitioned through each of their departments, William delivered several great elements of feedback and praise when the teams outpaced their metrics and key performance indicators (KPIs). However, he also asked several, well-placed yet cutting questions when they fell short. Anil listened into these moments, leaning into the feedback, as William pressed one of his vice presidents about the quarterly miss of a key result associated with a large organizational objective. Anil was caught completely off-guard. To him, he was completely unaware of the key result miss, nor did he have any advanced warning of this miss even being in their slides, despite having access to the deck weeks before the quarterly business review. When William finally summarized his action plan and directed the feedback to Anil as the leader of the team, he reacted.

In this perceived pivotal moment of crisis, Anil's instinctual response was to deflect responsibility onto his vice president's subordinates, doing so in front of William. This public passing of blame was not just a reaction to being blindsided; it was a desperate bid to salvage his own reputation. However, this strategy backfired spectacularly. His immediate manager, Haruto, recognizing the escalating tension and potential damage to team dynamics, came off mute on the call and intervened. The advice was clear and direct: Anil was to step back, take the time to thoroughly understand the situation from his vice presidents, and evaluate the remedial steps they had already initiated. This counsel was rooted in a trust in their expertise and an understanding of the broader picture. Unfortunately, by attempting to shift blame reactively and publicly as a result of his surprise and lack of preparation, Anil unwittingly confirmed the very perceptions of inadequacy he feared most. Instead of demonstrating leadership and control, his actions illuminated a lack of confidence and teamwork, casting him in the very light of incompetence he sought to escape. This incident became a stark illustration of the counterproductive nature of blame-shifting and the importance of fostering a culture of collective accountability and support and above all preparedness.

After the disastrous leadership meeting, Anil, in an attempt to rectify the situation, convened a meeting with all his vice presidents to delve into the problem at hand. He never wanted to be blindsided like that again. However, what was intended as a briefing to gain a comprehensive understanding of the current state quickly devolved into a series of individual inquisitions. Anil, driven by a need to identify the root of the failure, embarked on a fault-finding mission, questioning every decision made by his vice presidents. His approach was not one of seeking clarity or solutions, but rather pinpointing blame. He probed with the wrong questions, focusing his investigation on culpability rather than expressing trust in his vice presidents' actions and decisions.

This approach created an environment of defensiveness and mistrust. Anil held his team to an unrealistic standard of perfection, scrutinizing past decisions with the benefit of hindsight rather than using the opportunity to foster growth and provide guidance. His inability to recognize the value of collaborative problem-solving and support led to the issuance of disjointed, tactical, and reactionary commands. These directives not only undermined the vice presidents' autonomy and expertise but also exacerbated the situation. Over time, it became evident that Anil's actions, far from resolving the issue, had indeed made it worse, illustrating the detrimental impact of a leadership style marred by blame and lack of trust.

The Scourge of the "Stand Up"

As with any fault-finding activity, nothing productive was achieved. As a result, Anil quickly established a series of detailed "stand ups" in which the minutiae of the vice president's teams would be surfaced and discussed. An obvious immediate reaction to the negative outcomes of being surprised, this level of micromanagement led to Anil diving deep into the machinations of tactical tasks and activities of his organization in an effort to grasp all aspects of the situation to avoid being surprised ever again. This level of scrutiny quickly proved to be untenable and unproductive. It resulted in sessions where unreasonable questions, inspections, and inserting Anil's perspectives into context-rich situations served more as a disruption, leaving his own vice presidents to defend their team's execution amidst a backdrop of context that he could never hope to attain, nor should he.

Eventually, the stand-up cycle continued, dragging teams from their tasks only to report fractured superdetailed tasks, steps and information to Anil who for very good reasons, had little to no understanding of the information at such a fine-grained level. Once the demands of Anil's day job caught up to him, he slowly began to sacrifice attending the stand ups until he stopped completely, leaving his vice presidents and their teams in a lurch, holding a superfluous stand up that was redundant to their already well-oiled pattern of execution.

This left the cycle to refresh anew, where his vice presidents awaited the next time they would hear the same dreaded question.

"How is this the first time I'm hearing about this?"

The Archetype Defined

The Surprised manager archetype epitomizes leaders who are perpetually caught off-guard by information, developments, or problems that they should reasonably be aware of. This type of manager frequently expresses astonishment or confusion over updates and issues, often asking a single notorious question amidst frustration and misplaced indignation.

"Why am I just learning about this now?"

They often ask this despite prior discussions or briefings. Characterized by a seeming disconnect from the ongoing flow of information within their team or organization, The Surprised manager often struggles with staying afloat as their teams execute, frequently representing their inability to be informed in disruptive ways that repeatedly inadvertently undermine team morale and efficiency. Their constant surprise not only highlights a potential gap in their engagement with the team's activities but also puts into question their ability to manage and foresee challenges effectively. This archetype serves as a cautionary tale about the importance of staying informed, engaging in proactive communication, and the continuous cultivation of a supportive and transparent team environment.

This question, "Why am I just hearing about this now?" often becomes a scathing source of frustration for team members, embodying a deeper failure of leadership that transcends mere surprise. In the dynamic landscape of any project or organization, surprises and unforeseen issues are par for the course—a reality that every effective leader understands and prepares for. However, for The Surprised manager, being caught off-guard not only signifies a personal loss of control but also a perceived diminution of their capability in the eyes of peers and superiors. This perception triggers a defensive instinct, leading to a reactionary rather than a responsive leadership style. In an effort to deflect blame and preserve their standing, The Surprised manager may inadvertently undermine their team by publicly criticizing or blaming subordinates. This approach not only damages team morale but also erodes trust, highlighting a critical flaw in leadership: the inability to accept responsibility and foster a culture of collective problem-solving and accountability.

The Surprised manager is also often besieged by challenging workloads. In many cases, combined with an inability to manage significant large-scale programs that place outsized demands on their time and require significant attention, these managers often miss critical information, leading to them being surprised in highly inconvenient situations. This can lead to conversations like the following one.

Anil: "How is this the first time I'm hearing about this?"

Vice President: "You remember during our last one-on-one last week, I reviewed this with you? I also sent you an email and an instant message about this topic and what I planned to do about it. You never replied."

Anil: "You can't just IM me about things of this magnitude."

Vice President: "Here is the email that I sent to you about this topic last week. I'll forward it to you again so it's at the top of your inbox."

Anil: "Oh, I didn't see this … Let me read this and get back to you."

According to research, communication breakdowns can significantly reduce team productivity, impacting overall performance and efficiency.[*] In this case, the communication breakdown is an inability of the manager to receive and process the signals being sent by their team to properly prepare them for a future event or outcome. The team is sending, sometimes in excess of normal levels of communication, but the more signals that are sent, the more they seemingly go unprocessed by The Surprised manager. This can be a direct result of the volume of signals (i.e., communication, demands, and requests) they deal with.

Core Analysis

At the core of the "Why am I just hearing about this now?" scenario lies a tumultuous mix of emotions that plague The Surprised manager. Embarrassment is often the first to surface, stemming from the stark realization of being out of the loop on a critical issue. This is not merely a question of missing information but a profound self-reckoning about their grasp on the team's pulse and a project's trajectory. Coupled with this embarrassment is a deep-seated frustration, a gnawing feeling that morphs into a sense of betrayal. The manager might start to wonder, "Why didn't anyone tell me?" This thought can quickly spiral into darker territory, where the absence of prior warning is seen not as an oversight but potentially as a deliberate act by subordinates or peers—

_____

[*]Springer, Challenges and Barriers in Virtual Teams (Springer, 2020).

perhaps even a conspiracy to undermine their authority or embarrass them in front of their peers and superiors.

Alongside these emotional whirlwinds is the daunting realization of lack of control. Discovering a significant issue that has unfolded "on their watch" without their knowledge shakes the very foundation of what they believe their role entails. It's a sobering moment that brings into sharp view the limitations of their oversight and the fallibility of their leadership. The magnitude of such surprises not only questions their competence but also leaves them scrambling, unprepared to address the issue effectively. This cocktail of emotions—embarrassment, frustration, betrayal, and a profound sense of losing grip—paints a complex picture of the internal turmoil faced by The Surprised manager. It underscores the intricate challenges of leadership and the critical importance of fostering open, proactive communication within teams, which is a common area of improvement for a lot of archetypes.

Coping Strategies

Navigating the challenges posed by The Surprised manager archetype requires a strategic approach focused on anticipation, documentation, and regular communication. Anticipating potential areas of surprise in your managers enables you to proactively address concerns and prepare comprehensive updates for leadership and broader stakeholders. Demystifying and communicating the problems or challenges and the recommended ways to deal with them collaboratively and through conversation is the first coping mechanism.

Secondarily, documenting all forms of communication and decisions creates a reliable record to reference, reducing misunderstandings and holding all parties accountable. Establishing a routine of frequent and structured updates ensures that the manager remains informed and engaged, mitigating the likelihood of surprise and fostering a transparent working relationship.

While documentation is important, it's also important to create an aperture where the information can be given proper attention to where it's understood. Seeking a balance between documentation, early and often, and ensuring that the manager understands the documentation ahead of critical time horizons is the art form. Recall in the aforementioned example how even though there was adequate documentation and a track record of informing Anil to avoid surprise, the outcome was the same undesirable impact of being surprised, despite the information being sent to and presented to him. Documentation is important, but it's a part of the solution, not the whole thing.

Talk. It. Out

The first coping strategy for effectively managing The Surprised manager archetype involves setting clear and concise explanations and expectations. This approach is centered on fostering an environment of open dialogue and mutual understanding between you and your manager. In this open dialogue, the goal is to help your manager "look down the road" at potential challenges and the ways in which you or your team will respond to them when they arise. Essentially, your goal is to mitigate any surprises by helping your manager see them coming. By proactively discussing potential occurrences and outcomes, both positive and negative, and helping managers weigh the pros and cons of different decisions, you can significantly reduce the occurrence of surprises. This strategy not only aids in aligning expectations but also empowers managers to make informed decisions, thereby enhancing the team's ability to navigate challenges and achieve its objectives with a shared vision.

Talking it out brings context and life to the true impact of decisions, developments, and potential areas of caution or hazard. By talking to your manager in concise, structured terms, including a background of the problem, challenge or development, key considerations and alternatives, and your recommended path, you can provide your manager with the context, stakes, and an opportunity to support the selected course of action. Typically, few of us have as much time as we'd like to with our managers on a weekly or even a monthly basis. As a result, radical prioritization based on an assessment of the "blast radius" of a specific topic is important. In this case, the potential surprise or situation with the largest blast radius comes first, followed by others in decreasing order of magnitude.

When implementing this coping strategy, there are some key successful tactics that must be observed.

Employing empathy in your interactions with your manager creates a common ground of understanding that makes them more receptive to your suggestions. By genuinely acknowledging and empathizing with their challenges and perspectives, you foster an environment of trust and openness. This emotional connection is crucial; it shifts your manager into a state more amenable to listening and considering your ideas. Conversely, if you bypass this step and rely solely on logic and reason without engaging emotionally, you are likely to encounter resistance, as the necessary rapport and mutual respect may not be established. Thus, empathy is not just beneficial but essential for paving the way toward effective communication and change. It's also important to note that the majority of recommendations in this book revolve around overcoming resistance to change by using this technique.

Never have a meeting with your manager without an agenda. Having meandering and mostly pleasant conversations with your leader are important as they help you both form a lasting collaborative relationship, but in terms of making sure they're not surprised or caught unawares, you require a specific framework for outcome-based discussions.

Never have a meeting with your manager without prescribed outcomes for each agenda item. These can range from simple FYIs, warnings, context and understanding, education, support in your prescribed path or action, or a combination of all of these.

After verbally talking it out with your manager, indicate how you will send a follow-up communication (via a channel of your choice that you know your manager pays attention to) summarizing and confirming your mutual understanding of the topics you discussed.

Putting It Into Practice

In the wake of a project review meeting with William, the Chief Information Officer (CIO), where Anil expressed shock over missed deadlines that he was previously informed about, Maria, one of Anil's vice presidents, decides to address the communication gap directly.

> **Maria:** "Anil, I noticed there was some surprise on your end regarding the project timelines and our KPI misses during our meeting with William. I think there might be a better way for us to ensure we're all aligned on these updates in the future."
>
> **Anil:** "I just don't get how I missed these updates, Maria. It feels like I'm always the last to know, even when I'm trying to stay on top of everything."
>
> **Maria:** "That must be really unsettling. I know I hate it when you're caught unawares, and I'm committed to preventing that from happening again. What if we set aside time each week for a brief one-on-one? You could share your expectations and priorities, and I can provide real-time updates on our progress and any challenges. This way, we can address potential issues together before they escalate."
>
> **Anil:** "Maria, my schedule is already packed. I don't know if I can fit in another regular meeting."
>
> **Maria:** "I understand that time is a major constraint for you, Anil. However, these brief check-ins could actually save you time in the long run by avoiding the disruptions that come from being surprised. Plus, they'd ensure you're always prepared, especially in front of senior management like today. Think of this as an investment in your peace of mind and in maintaining control over the department's output."
>
> **Anil:** (*pausing to consider*) "Well, I can't afford to be the last to know, especially not in front of William. Go ahead and schedule these meetings, but make sure they're efficient and strictly timed; I need them to be focused and productive."
>
> **Maria:** "Absolutely, I'll prepare an agenda for each meeting in advance, and we'll stick to the key points. I'll also follow up with a brief summary via email, so you have a record of what was discussed, and any decisions made."

This conversation effectively illustrates how Maria uses emotional intelligence to navigate Anil's initial resistance to the idea of additional meetings. She empathizes with his feeling of unsettlement about being surprised and leverages this to propose a solution that aligns with his needs to stay informed and prepared. Maria's understanding of Anil's busy schedule and her assurance to keep the meetings efficient and productive addresses his concerns directly, making the proposal more appealing.

Furthermore, Maria's strategy to send follow-up communications aligns with the successful tactics outlined earlier: ensuring that every meeting has a clear agenda and defined outcomes and reinforcing discussions with written summaries. This approach not only enhances the structure and effectiveness of their communication but also builds a framework for ongoing dialogue that minimizes the risk of Anil being caught off-guard in the future.

Maria demonstrated how empathizing with Anil let her establish the fact that she truly understood Anil's frustrations, and his resulting emotions. Based on this mutual understanding, Maria was able to get Anil to a point where he was ready to listen to her suggestion. Her tactful handling of the situation illustrates how proactive measures, grounded in empathy and strategic planning, created room for him to establish a mechanism (scheduled meetings to Talk It Out) to help Anil avoid being surprised all the time.

Write. It. Down.

Coping with The Surprised manager archetype, who often expresses shock or unawareness of situations despite previous briefings, requires a proactive and documentation-based communication strategy. To navigate through the challenges posed by such managers, it is essential to meticulously document all interactions, decisions, and updates. Writing down details of meetings, conversations, and emails serves as a tangible record that can be referred back to when the manager claims ignorance or surprise. This practice not only safeguards your credibility but also encourages the manager to become more engaged and informed. Also note that what cuts down on this the most are preemptive conversations you have with your manager, prior to writing it down.

To effectively manage interactions with The Surprised manager and mitigate the risk of "executive forgetting," adopting a meticulous documentation practice is paramount. This involves transitioning from reliance solely on verbal communications (as described in the Talk It Out strategy earlier), which are inherently fleeting and susceptible to distortion, to a structured written record. Utilizing tools such as personal notes, Slack or Teams messages, and emails can serve as a tangible and permanent record of all communications and decisions.

Each written communication should be comprehensive, starting with a clear summary or title that captures the essence of the content. It should succinctly outline the issue or topic at hand, providing a brief yet thorough description. Including actionable alternatives and a recommendation within the document is crucial; this not only presents a problem but also offers solutions, making it easier for the manager to make informed decisions. Moreover, it's essential to enrich these documents with key metadata: the date and time of the communication, the personnel involved in the discussions, and a summary of the outcomes and next steps. This level of detail ensures that there's a clear, traceable record of the decision-making process, which can be referenced in future discussions or when the manager exhibits signs of surprise or forgetfulness. Through diligent application of these practices, employees can create a robust framework for communication that significantly reduces the likelihood of misunderstandings and reinforces accountability.

When dealing with The Surprised manager archetype, who frequently shows signs of forgetfulness or shock over previously discussed matters, it is crucial not only to document interactions meticulously but also to distribute this documentation strategically. Beyond sending these summaries just to your manager (who likely will not read them), consider sharing them with relevant peers—including those of your manager—when the subject matter is appropriate. This practice creates a broader council of accountability.

By circulating documented interactions among a wider audience, you leverage a collective awareness that naturally fosters a more attentive and engaged environment from participants, especially your manager. This approach can be particularly effective because it subtly introduces a layer of peer review and oversight. Knowing that their colleagues, especially their equals, are in the loop and can see the documented interactions, often motivates managers to pay closer attention and stay more informed. Because of the expanded audience, they become less likely to claim ignorance on matters that have been clearly documented and shared. This not only helps in keeping everyone on the same page but also reinforces the importance of accountability and reduces the potential for miscommunication. Employing this strategy not only safeguards your credibility but also enhances the collective responsibility within the team, promoting a culture where valuable information is consistently acknowledged and acted upon.

Putting It Into Practice

The following example demonstrates a recommended strategy that can be extremely useful in the "Write. It. Down" coping strategy. In this example, one of Anil's vice presidents are proactively using this strategy to anticipate Anil's past behavior of surprise and to attempt to mitigate it with an approach and documentation so it's clear. The strategy involves constructing documentation, inclusive of all stakeholders, concerned peers and parties, which outlines the importance of the upcoming meeting and the weight of the session and its stakes. It then shows the challenge or problem, referring to a time when the topic was previously discussed and, finally, focuses on the plan of action and acquiring Anil's tacit approval.

To: Anil
CC: [Immediate Peers], [Stakeholders]

Note by distributing this communication to others, it helps the collaboration between stakeholders and concerned parties by establishing a cohort for accountability. This way, everyone can see and benefit from the cohesive preemptive tactic being used to prevent Anil from being surprised during the meeting. It creates a chorus of people that "think the same thing and say the same thing."

Subject: Upcoming CIO Meeting—Preparedness and Strategic Recommendations

Hi Anil,

In anticipation of our meeting with William [the CIO] scheduled for [Date and Time], I wanted to share a comprehensive overview of the key points we plan to discuss, along with actionable alternatives and my recommendation to ensure that we are fully prepared and aligned. I'm including [Immediate Peers], [Stakeholders] for awareness as I've worked with them on this topic and this note will get us all on the same page.

> Note how, in this introduction, we are setting the scope of the communication and its importance. Also note how we are proactively mitigating any angst as to why other parties are included on this email by calling it out boldly in advance that we are cc'ing other concerned parties in the interest of collaboration. Calling this out and explaining why these parties were included help mitigate any feelings of angst or "tattling" Anil might feel associated with who this message was sent to.

As we discussed in our meeting on [Date and Time], I wanted to summarize what we agreed on.

> Note how we're reminding Anil that we've already discussed this on a specific date and time, and he should be primed to recall the information.

Summary/Title: Strategic Initiative Review for CIO Meeting

Note the bold headings to draw the reader's attention to the information they need to retain. When people read email, they largely scan for headings and read only the first few words or sentences beneath the heading. However, the reason this is effective is because it structures the message in Anil's mind so that when it's heard again, it's familiar, thereby avoiding surprise.

Description of the Issue/Topic

We will be presenting our proposal to deal with the new challenge that our lines of business are having and to align them with the strategic initiative, which aims to enhance our IT infrastructure and digital capabilities. This initiative is crucial for our department's future success and requires the CIO's endorsement. Without it, we won't be able to maintain our market competitiveness and may fall into second place behind organizations that directly compete with us.

> Note how we paint the stakes of this recommendation and outline the startling negative outcomes if we don't act to address this issue.

Actionable Alternatives

> Here we're using a header to define what the options are. This is a preemptive measure to prevent Anil from being surprised that other options or courses of action were not already considered. If this isn't successful, Anil will most likely engage in "deconstruction" during the real meeting, tossing out alternatives that are aged, were already considered and discarded or out of date. This will serve to destabilize his own vice president's recommendations and present a fractured and unrefined course of action to the CIO. This section avoids this.

Accelerated Timeline Implementation: Fast-track the initiative by Q4, requiring increased budget and resources.

Phased Rollout: Implement the initiative in stages, allowing for adjustments and minimizing initial resource allocation.

Recommendation

Given the critical nature of this initiative and potential resource constraints, I recommend adopting the phased rollout approach. This strategy balances progress with flexibility, allowing us to demonstrate early wins to stakeholders and adjust based on feedback and outcomes.

> Note how Anil will probably not read this far down in the message, nor completely take the time to understand all the alternatives, but it's vital for documentation indicating that it was verbally discussed, proposed and talked about.

Outcomes and Next Steps

As discussed with the team, in particular [Peers and other stakeholders who share the same conclusion], I propose we finalize our presentation materials by [Specific Date] and schedule a rehearsal meeting by [Another Date] to ensure that our messaging is cohesive and impactful. Your feedback on the proposed recommendation and any adjustments to our approach would be invaluable.

> Here we are indicating that we have vetted this proposal with other peers and stakeholders. Also note that we are embracing positive collaboration by seeking Anil's input, prior to the session. This achieves the critical outcome going into the meeting where Anil is saying the same thing and reinforcing the vice president's message, instead of being surprised by it and publicly deconstructing it, thereby becoming an adversary for his own team members due to his surprise.

I believe that by following this structured approach, we can mitigate potential surprises and present a well-considered proposal to the CIO. Your insights and directives on this matter would greatly influence our preparation and eventual success.

Please let me know if you have any issues or suggestions with how we plan to proceed.

This statement is crucial. Most people when reading email read what's "before the fold," meaning what fits on a device's screen before scrolling. They then scroll aggressively through the bulk of lengthy content and then scan the last paragraph and sentence for asks or action items for them. In this sentence, we're indicating that unless Anil proactively responds and alters the planned course as outlined in this message, the course will continue. This is a powerful sentence because it places Anil in a position where his inaction or lack of response constitutes compliance, thereby freeing the team to proceed. If there ever is a circumstance where they are indeed surprised (and it can happen despite this coping mechanism), this becomes a crucial documented pivot point to refer back to.

Even if Anil gets to this point, having scrolled through the majority of the message without absorbing the details, it may encourage him to go back and read through again, this time with more scrutiny, and attempt to truly understand the full context and details of the email.

Thanks,
[Vice President]

Adopting a disciplined approach to communication and decision documentation is crucial when dealing with The Surprised manager archetype, especially in preparation for significant discussions. Incorporating the Talk it Out strategy by setting up regular check-ins or briefings ensures that managers are consistently informed, which, when followed by meticulous documentation and strategic distribution of these documents to a carefully selected audience—including peers and other stakeholders—reinforces the shared information and maintains collective awareness. Together, these practices create a robust framework that not only equips the manager with necessary information to avoid surprise but it also cultivates a culture of accountability and precision within the team. This systematic approach significantly enhances overall performance, promotes transparency, minimizes surprises, and ensures a smoother, more productive work environment.

Summing It Up

A balanced approach to communicating verbally with your manager, in a structured way, followed by a written summary of the directions, conclusions, and action items, focused on readability will help you deal with The Surprised manager archetype. The goal is to utilize these coping strategies to mitigate surprise by using a multichannel approach (both verbal and written) to remove any chance of them being surprised.

1. **Anticipate Managerial Surprises**: Anticipating potential surprises involves understanding your manager's concerns and priorities. By predicting areas that might cause surprise, you can prepare and address these issues proactively, minimizing the impact of unexpected revelations.

2. **Structured Communication**: Structured communication entails regular, planned interactions that provide clear and concise updates to your manager. This approach ensures that your manager stays informed and can significantly reduce the frequency of surprises.

3. **Documentation Is Key**: Keeping detailed records of decisions, meetings, and discussions creates a tangible reference that can clarify expectations and responsibilities. This documentation serves as a safeguard against forgetfulness and misunderstanding, enhancing accountability for all involved.

4. **Create an Information Aperture**: Ensuring that documentation is not only provided but also understood by the manager is crucial. It involves tailoring the presentation of information to ensure it captures the manager's attention and is comprehensible, fostering better decision-making. Also making sure to distribute the documentation to your manager and to their peers ensures a dimension of accountability and visibility that may encourage your manager to pay attention to your documentation.

5. **Seek Balance in Notification**: Judiciously deciding what information to convey and when to convey it is essential. Balancing the urgency and relevance of information helps in effectively managing the flow of communication without overwhelming or underinforming your manager.

6. **Utilize Verbal and Written Summaries**: Following up significant verbal exchanges with written summaries helps reinforce understanding and alignment. These summaries ensure that both parties have a clear, shared record of discussions and agreements, reducing the likelihood of discrepancies.

7. **Schedule Regular Updates**: Establishing a routine for frequent updates provides a steady stream of information to the manager. This consistent communication fosters transparency and keeps the manager actively engaged with the team's progress and challenges.

8. **Empower Managers with Solution Options**: When presenting issues, also providing viable solutions empowers your manager to make informed decisions. This proactive approach encourages a collaborative problem-solving environment and demonstrates initiative and foresight.

9. **Promote Mutual Growth**: Using these strategies not only aids in managing upward but also supports mutual development between you and your manager. It's about building a relationship that fosters growth, understanding, and respect in both directions.

10. **Reflect and Adjust**: Continuous evaluation of communication and documentation strategies is essential for improvement. Reflecting on what works and what doesn't allow for adjustments to be made, ensuring that the approach remains effective and responsive to the needs of both you and your manager.

Note that it is rare that a manager will apply the appropriate amount of time and energy to understand a complex, impactful, and high-stakes topic that is entirely introduced through a written communication channel (i.e., email or instant messaging). Conversely, simple verbal warnings, confirmations, and touchpoints without a record enforcing the discussion and any conclusions or actions will likely slip from your managers "RAM stack" (i.e., their temporary working memory), leading to surprise later, and frustration on your part. Through the application of these coping strategies, you should rarely encounter yourself saying "I already told you about this. How can you not know?"

CHAPTER 2

The Emergency Broadcaster

Background

In the dim light of the early morning, Amina's phone buzzed insistently on the nightstand, tearing through the silence with the urgency of a Slack notification. She sat upright when she realized it was from her manager (an executive vice president). It was a message punctuated with a sense of urgency that instantly set Amina's heart racing. The message inquired pointedly about her team's preparations for a high stakes meeting later in the day, a meeting where several of her team of vice presidents were slated to speak. Her manager was keen on verifying the key content in her team's presentations, emphasizing the importance of being fully prepared for what was clearly a critical gathering.

The blood drained from Amina's face as she read and reread the message. Panic set in; she had no recollection of such a meeting, let alone which members of her team were presenting. The realization hit her like a ton of bricks—she was unprepared, a fact that sent her into a frenzied scramble. With the clock ticking ominously toward dawn, she hastily composed a message to her team as fast as her thumbs allowed, calling for an emergency meeting at 7:30 a.m. Her mind raced, ignoring the implications of her decision on her team's personal morning routines—children needed to be dropped off at school, morning jogs were a sacred ritual for some, and others had meticulously timed commutes. All these routines would now be disrupted, sacrificed at the altar of a fire drill meeting summoned by Amina's oversight.

The Zoom meeting room, usually a space of collaborative energy, took on a different aura that morning. People joined from the back of Ubers, trains or buses, or from their cars with their kids screaming in the background. Some even had to juggle their phones and coffees as they joined from Starbucks as they headed into the office. It was filled with the palpable tension of disrupted routines and the underlying frustration of a team pulled away from their personal lives. Amina could see the fatigue and irritation on her team's faces, a silent testament to the cost of her chaotic management style. The hastily arranged gathering, meant to salvage a situation born from a lack of foresight, underscored a pattern all too familiar—Amina's struggle to navigate the demands of leadership without a clear strategic direction, leaving her team to navigate the fallout of her emergency broadcasts.

In a well-intentioned but misguided attempt to mitigate disruptions to her vice presidents' schedules for the rest of the day, Amina scheduled the early meeting, believing it would spare them the hassle of calendar readjustments. Contrary to her expectations, this decision had the adverse effect of significantly inconveniencing her team. It pulled them out of their personal commitments and morning routines, leading to frustration as they were forced to revisit content that Amina had been sent days or even weeks in advance, content she should have been familiar with.

This incident marked the third emergency meeting called by Amina in a single month, highlighting an increasingly common practice within her management style. Her team's growing frustration was palpable, reflecting a pattern of reactive leadership that prioritized immediate fixes over strategic planning without consideration for the team's work–life balance.

The Archetype Defined

Introducing The Emergency Broadcaster: a management archetype that thrives on the adrenaline of urgency and the thrill of the last-minute save. This type of manager navigates the workplace like a ship captain in a perpetual storm, often steering the team from one crisis to another with a flair for dramatic, impromptu calls to action. Characterized by a reactive approach, The Emergency Broadcaster is typically blindsided by foreseeable challenges—issues and deadlines that, with proper foresight, could have been addressed smoothly. This frequent happening results in the emergency broadcast, a disruptive, shrill and chaotic call to action amidst a well-planned set of task execution by teams.

In the world of The Emergency Broadcaster, your workday may be typically punctuated with urgent meetings and sudden, critical demands, disrupting the flow of planned activities and injecting a chronic sense of chaos into you and your team's routine. This style of management often originates from a mix of poor planning, insufficient oversight, and a propensity to overlook or forget essential details until the moment they reach a boiling point. While they may view their high-stakes, high-pressure tactics as a strategy to foster agility and keep the team alert, it often results in a workplace where stress levels are as high as the stakes.

Research indicates that constant urgency (and its ensuing miscommunication) created by management significantly increases employee stress levels, leading to substantial drops in productivity.[*] This heightened stress not only impacts individual well-being but also hampers overall team efficiency and morale. While there's nothing wrong with facilitating a sense of urgency when the team has to perform, unanticipated and frequent emergency broadcasts can inadvertently create a high-pressure environment that diminishes employees' ability to perform at their best.

For teams under the watch of an Emergency Broadcaster, every day feels like a trial by fire, where personal time and well-organized schedules are sacrificed on the altar of emergency broadcasts (urgent meetings, emails, and messages that call on all hands to stop and pivot at the last second). This archetype's approach not only tests the resilience of the team but also poses significant challenges to maintaining morale and preventing burnout. If you find yourself nodding in weary recognition, stay tuned; the following pages are dedicated to mastering the turbulent waves stirred up by The Emergency Broadcaster, transforming potential workplace chaos into a navigable course toward calm and structured productivity.

Examining the previous narrative, Amina, a managing vice president, perfectly encapsulates this dynamic. Her intentions, though

---

[*]Workforce.com, 2023, "The State of (Mis)Communication."

aimed at preserving her team's daytime productivity, inadvertently reveal a deeper issue—a reactive rather than proactive approach to management. By pulling her team out of their personal commitments for emergency reviews of content long since provided, Amina exemplifies the critical flaw in The Emergency Broadcaster archetype.

Just like an emergency broadcast message (or cellular carrier alert), this archetype's behavior interrupts everyone, regardless of what they are doing and forces them into being captive participants in an often remedial exercise. While emergencies in business are as inevitable as the setting sun, the frequent, preemptive 7:30 a.m. meetings (or a similarly offensive calendar time) become the defining hallmark of this archetype. They signal a deeper need for improved organizational skills, strategic foresight, and a genuine respect for the personal and professional boundaries of the team. Addressing this archetype's challenges is essential, not just for the well-being of the team, but for fostering a sustainable, productive work environment where emergencies are the exception, not the rule.

Core Analysis

The Emergency Broadcaster archetype often emerges from a swirling mix of personal management styles and organizational pressures, far surpassing simple unpreparedness. At the heart of their approach lies an instinctive response to stress—when deadlines loom or crises erupt, these managers spring into action, driven by the belief that immediate, decisive responses are the only solution. This reactive mode often skips over more measured strategies, such as reviewing past communications or considering long-term impacts, which might provide a smoother resolution. It's as if, in their world, every fire must be doused with a bucket of urgency, often without checking if it's just a campfire needing a gentle sprinkle.

On a deeper level, some of these leaders have come to believe in the effectiveness of their methods through past experiences. Perhaps they've seen success when capable subordinates are dragged out of position at the last minute to swarm on a particular challenge or problem. This creates a self-reinforcing cycle where urgency equates to efficiency.

Imagine a manager who views every project like defusing a bomb— timer ticking down, red wires waiting to be snipped. It's thrilling, sure, but it's hardly a sustainable way to run a team. The drama may be compelling, but the constant high-stakes environment can wear down even the most resilient teams, turning everyday tasks into episodes of a suspense thriller. If you resonate with this description, read on, but also check out The Firefighter management archetype later in the book.

The backdrop of organizational culture also plays a pivotal role. In environments where a lack of robust organizational systems for regular communication, expectation setting, updates and risk assessments exist, it creates a perfect storm for The Emergency Broadcaster's behavior to be a routine way of getting things done. Without clear protocols, these managers often find themselves in the dark until the eleventh hour, forced to broadcast emergencies as a way of navigating through the organizational fog. It's a chaotic dance that underscores a need for better tools and training in proactive management, ensuring that the ship is steered with a calm hand rather than racing ahead on stormy seas.

Understanding the root cause of this behavior is crucial for addressing and mitigating its impact on the team. It involves fostering an environment where planning and foresight are valued over reactive measures. Encouraging The Emergency Broadcaster to adopt more strategic planning techniques and improve communication channels can help prevent the cascade of disruptions caused by their impromptu meetings. Helping them build confidence in their leadership style without relying on emergency measures can lead to more thoughtful and less intrusive decision-making.

Equipping yourself with strategies to cope with or adapt to working under The Emergency Broadcaster can empower you to maintain your work–life balance while still meeting professional obligations. This could include setting clear boundaries regarding availability, using documented communication to track and remind managers of previously shared information, and fostering a culture of mutual respect and understanding for personal time.

Coping Strategies

Dealing with The Emergency Broadcaster archetype—a manager prone to initiating urgent meetings, email, or other disruptive communications due to unforeseen issues—requires strong communication, effective boundary-setting, and proactive measures. Such managers typically operate on impulse, reacting to crises that could be better anticipated with foresight. To mitigate their disruptive impact, it's crucial to establish clear boundaries by explicitly defining your availability for meetings and urgent communications to maintain a balance between professional responsibilities and personal well-being, while allowing some flexibility. Additionally, if a meeting occurs outside your specified hours, creating a mechanism to catch up on what was discussed through summaries from attending colleagues will be critical. Reducing misunderstandings through advanced strategic outlooks and planning will also help reduce the need for emergency sessions, helping to foster a work environment that values strategic planning and respects both personal and professional time.

Set Clear Boundaries

Setting clear boundaries is crucial in mitigating the disruption caused by The Emergency Broadcaster management archetype. It involves a delicate balance between maintaining professional responsibilities and preserving personal well-being. While effective, this strategy carries risks, such as the possibility of missing essential information shared in an impromptu 7:30 a.m. meeting. The art of setting boundaries requires careful communication, consistent enforcement, and a readiness to deal with the consequences.

To implement clear boundaries, start by openly communicating your available hours for meetings and urgent communications. Be specific about the times when you are and aren't available, emphasizing the importance of respecting these boundaries to maintain productivity and work–life balance. It's essential to frame this conversation around the mutual benefits of such an arrangement, highlighting how it can lead to more focused work and better outcomes. Note that it isn't advisable to be completely inflexible and draw a hard line, but setting expectations around how difficult and unlikely it is to join these emergency meetings is the right balance.

Even though you are successful in setting key boundary expectations, choosing to set and enforce boundaries may still lead to challenging scenarios. You might face concerns about not being seen as a team player, fear of missing out on critical decisions or discussions, and perceptions of lacking commitment. These risks are real and require a strategic approach to navigate. Here are some steps that you can use, in combination with setting boundaries that often help in dealing with this manager archetype.

Demonstrate Commitment in Other Ways: Make it clear that your commitment to your work and team is unwavering, but that you believe this can be achieved more effectively with a balanced approach to urgent meetings and personal time. Show your dedication through the quality of your work and your contributions during agreed-upon hours.

Follow Up Proactively: If you decide to miss a meeting scheduled outside your available hours in observance of your boundaries, arrange to follow up with a colleague who attended to get a summary of what was discussed. This initiative shows that while you respect your boundaries, you remain committed to staying informed and contributing value.

Communicate Clearly and Respectfully: When informing your manager of your boundaries, do so respectfully and clearly. Explain the rationale behind your availability, focusing on how it benefits your productivity and the quality of your work. Offer solutions, such as alternative meeting times or asynchronous updates, to ensure you're not hindering the flow of critical information. The goal is to stem the instinct for your manager to expect that you will drop everything and jump on a call. By negotiating clear, scheduled times in which you can interact will stem the instinct of "The Emergency Broadcaster" to expect your attendance.

Deal With FOMO: The fear of missing out (FOMO) on important discussions or decisions can be mitigated by creating a culture of comprehensive meeting notes and shared summaries. Advocate for documentation of meetings and decisions, making it easier for all team members to stay informed, regardless of their ability to attend every meeting. Many meeting services now offer artificial intelligence (AI) agents that will automatically document, transcribe, and summarize meetings that you miss. The fear that you'll miss an opportunity, while others may get to take advantage of them is a significant foil to this coping strategy. It can erode your own ability to respect your boundaries if you aren't careful. Learn to work with these new meeting tools that automatically capture, summarize, and allow you to interact with meetings after they've happened to help you catch up (i.e., Microsoft Teams).

By effectively setting and maintaining clear boundaries, you can create a more sustainable work environment for yourself and potentially for others who may feel the same pressures but have been hesitant to speak up. This approach can lead to a shift in how emergency meetings are perceived and handled, encouraging more strategic planning and respect for personal time across the team.

In the end, while setting boundaries with The Emergency Broadcaster archetype may be challenging, it is a crucial step toward fostering a healthier work–life balance and demonstrating that high productivity can be achieved without sacrificing personal time and well-being. Remember that if you don't respect your boundaries, no one else will.

Putting It Into Practice

Claire is about to pass Amina in the hall at the end of the day on her way out of the office. As Amina approaches, Claire can tell she's furiously typing into her phone as she slowly walks down the hallway. After exchanging a polite hello, she stops Claire, shouting after her before she heads to the parking garage.

Amina: "Claire, we need to have an emergency meeting at 7:30 a.m. tomorrow. Haruto just threw a new initiative at us, and we need to strategize immediately."

Claire: "Amina, I heard rumors about this initiative a few weeks ago. Was this just dropped on you last minute?"

Amina: (*bristling*) "Yes, it was just confirmed late last night, and it's critical we address this now. I need everyone on board tomorrow morning."

Claire: "I understand the urgency, Amina, but I have a prior commitment to drop my kids off at daycare during that time. I've set clear boundaries around my morning availability for reasons like this. Can we possibly schedule this for a time when I'm available?"

Amina: "Claire, this is a critical situation. I need all hands on deck. Can't you make an exception just this once?"

Claire: "I'm committed to the team and the project, but maintaining a predictable schedule is crucial for balancing my professional and personal responsibilities. How about we move the meeting to 9 a.m.? This would allow me to be fully present and engaged, ensuring we have a productive session."

Amina: "That's too late. We need to act fast."

Claire: "I propose an alternative then. Let's record the meeting so I can review it immediately after my commitment. I can follow up with any inputs by mid-morning. This way, I stay informed, and we maintain the momentum without disrupting our set boundaries."

Amina: (*pausing to consider*) "Okay, that could work. Make sure you're caught up before noon and ready to contribute. I'll have the meeting recorded, and we can align on your inputs later."

Claire: "Thank you, Amina. I appreciate the flexibility. I'll ensure I'm up to speed and ready to add value as soon as I'm back. Also, I'll arrange for a summary from my colleague who will be present at the meeting to ensure nothing is missed."

This conversation exemplifies how Claire successfully navigates through setting clear boundaries while maintaining her commitment to the team. By offering practical solutions such as rescheduling and utilizing meeting recordings, Claire demonstrates how to manage professional responsibilities effectively alongside personal commitments. Amina's initial resistance highlights a common challenge in workplace dynamics, but Claire's persistent yet respectful insistence on boundary-setting shows that it is possible to balance urgent work demands with personal life, thereby fostering a more sustainable work environment. Additionally, Amina has learned that Claire, while a valuable team player, seldom compromises on her boundaries.

Prevent the Forest Fires

One of the most effective ways to manage the Emergency Broadcaster is through proactive planning and communication. Think of it as preventing a forest fire: if you clear the underbrush and identify potential hotspots before the dry season hits, you can prevent the blaze from ever starting. Similarly, helping your manager look ahead and anticipate key meetings, commitments, and potential issues well in advance can stop crises before they ignite.

> **Preventative Check-Ins:** Schedule preventative check-ins with your manager, ideally during quieter periods between crises. Use these moments to capture their attention in short, focused bursts. Review upcoming projects, milestones, and key meetings, making sure your manager is aware of what's on the horizon. These sessions should be brief and to the point, ensuring that they fit into your manager's busy schedule without overwhelming them. While it may be challenging to secure time with your manager, emphasize the value of these check-ins as proactive measures to prevent emergencies, framing them as a way to avoid the forest fire rather than responding to it after it has already started.
>
> **Documentation Follow Up:** Follow up these planning sessions with detailed documentation. Create a shared calendar or project management tool where all key dates, commitments, and deadlines are clearly marked. Ensure that this information is easily

accessible and regularly updated. This way, when your manager is encouraged to research before sounding the alarm, they have a reliable resource to consult. A well-maintained documentation system can provide the necessary calm and clarity, reducing the impulse to ring the alarm bell unnecessarily. Be sure to walk your manager through the simple ways they can quickly turn to this resource when a potential emergency starts to get them the best information possible.

Utilize Technology: Leverage technology to keep information at your manager's fingertips. Tools like shared online calendars, project management software (such as Trello or Asana), and automated reminders can help keep your manager informed and organized. Set up notifications for upcoming deadlines and meetings to ensure that nothing slips through the cracks. Encourage your manager to use these tools regularly to stay on top of their responsibilities.

By implementing these proactive strategies, you can begin to help your manager adopt a more forward-thinking approach, reducing the frequency and impact of emergency broadcasts. This not only keeps your manager better prepared and informed but also fosters a more stable and productive work environment for the entire team. Through consistent effort and clear communication, you can transform the reactive tendencies of The Emergency Broadcaster into a more control-led and strategic leadership style.

Putting It Into Practice

Claire understood that proactive prevention is key to managing many undesirable manager archetypes, and The Emergency Broadcaster is no different. Anticipating trouble and taking early action can prevent crises from occurring. With this in mind, Claire decided to have a preemptive discussion with Amina about the upcoming Quarterly Business Review (QBR) with William, the CIO.

Claire: "Amina, can we talk for a minute about the upcoming QBR with William? It's scheduled for next month, and I think we should start preparing now."

Amina: (*sighing*) "What now, Claire? We're already swamped. What's the issue this time?"

Claire: "I understand, but this is important. I've been reviewing our key objectives and key results (OKRs), and there are a few potential trouble spots that might come up during the session. I thought it would be better to address them proactively rather than be caught off guard."

Amina: "Great. Just what I needed. More bad news. What exactly are we looking at?"

Claire: "Well, our customer satisfaction metric is below target, and we've missed a couple of key milestones on the new platform implementation. If we start addressing these now, we can frame our narrative constructively and even take some corrective actions to improve our metrics before the meeting."

Amina: (*frustrated*) "I can't believe we're in this situation again. Why am I only hearing about this now?"

Claire: "I know it's not ideal, but we have time to turn this around. I've set up a real-time dashboard where you can track our OKRs. My team is updating it regularly with the latest data. If we focus on the areas that need improvement now, we can present a more positive story during the QBR."

Amina: (*softening a bit*) "Okay, show me this dashboard."

Claire: (*pulling up the dashboard on her laptop*) "Here it is. As you can see, it gives a clear overview of where we stand on all our key metrics. We can use this to monitor our progress and make adjustments as needed. I suggest we check in one last time a few days before the meeting to ensure we're on track and ready to present."

Amina: "Alright, this does look useful. But we need to make sure this doesn't happen again. We can't keep scrambling at the last minute."

Claire: "Absolutely. That's why these proactive check-ins and using the dashboard are crucial. They help us stay ahead of potential issues and prevent these last-minute emergencies. If we maintain this approach, we can keep everything on track and reduce the stress on everyone."

This type of management coping strategy—proactive prevention and anticipation—is key to dealing with many of the archetypes discussed in this book. By scheduling preventative check-ins, maintaining detailed documentation, and leveraging technology, you can prevent reactive tendencies and instead create space for your manager to learn how to focus on controlled, strategic leadership. This approach helps managers stay informed and prepared, fostering a more stable and productive work environment.

Establish an Emergency Protocol

Emergencies are going to happen. There will be last-minute presentation requests, managers will be put on the spot and require instant support when they're in the hot seat, and deadlines and goalposts will be moved (typically forward, not backward). Given these constants, when dealing with an Emergency Broadcaster, it's essential to have a robust protocol in place for handling crises. This not only helps manage the situation efficiently but also reduces the stress and disruption caused by sudden team-wide emergency broadcasts, and ensuing chaotic actions that are detrimental to team harmony and cohesion. By establishing a "break glass in case of emergency" strategy, you can prevent the mad scramble to assemble all hands and instead rely on a structured approach involving the right personnel in a much smaller and focused manner. This protocol could include a checklist of steps to take, key contacts to notify, and resources to consult. Having a predefined plan can help manage the situation calmly and efficiently, reducing the stress and disruption caused by unexpected crises.

Establish Clear Areas of Responsibility: Create a list of team leaders or individuals and their documented scope of responsibilities and accountabilities. Having this list readily available to the manager will help when an emergency does arise. By identifying the key responsible or accountable individual or leader, The Emergency Broadcaster already has a limited number of people to approach, rather than the whole team. These individuals should have the authority and knowledge to intake, triage, and disposition the emergency effectively. Rotate this duty to ensure that no single person is overwhelmed and that there is always someone available to handle urgent issues.

Define Clear Communication Channels: Set up dedicated communication channels for emergency situations. This could be a text chain, a specific Slack channel, or a dedicated phone line. Ensure that all team members are aware of these channels and know how to use them. Quick and clear communication is critical in managing emergencies without causing unnecessary disruption. This will help The Emergency Broadcaster manager feel that there is a quick-response method of responding to perceived and unanticipated emergencies. You can also pin the areas of responsibility to this channel to help funnel the manager to the right accountable parties, keeping the blast radius of the emergency smaller and focused, but visible to other team members.

Guide the Right Questions: Equip responsible personnel with a set of guided questions to ask when an emergency is reported by The Emergency Broadcaster manager. These questions should help gather all necessary information quickly and accurately. In addition, they help invisibly shape the behavior of the manager to provide more focused, less panicked broadcasts, leading to a more measured way to intake and triage emergencies. The hope is that eventually, through persistent guidance, the manager may come to the predefined communication channel with this information. For example:

- What exactly is the issue, and how was it identified?

- What is the immediate impact, and what are the potential long-term consequences?
- Who needs to be involved in resolving this issue (leveraging to the accountable parties list from before)?
- What resources or tools are needed to address the problem?
- How soon is a resolution needed, and what are the timelines?

By implementing this structured emergency management protocol, you can effectively manage crises without causing widespread disruption. This approach not only helps in maintaining calm and efficiency during emergencies but also reassures the team that there is a clear plan in place, reducing anxiety and enhancing overall productivity. If enough guidance, via gentle suggestion and redirection to the protocol is employed, The Emergency Broadcaster will hopefully reduce or eliminate their instinctive behavior and utilize the new protocol instead.

Putting It Into Practice

Claire catches up with Amina after missing the last emergency 7:30 a.m. meeting due to her well-established boundaries. Understanding that proactive prevention is crucial, Claire decides to introduce Amina to a structured emergency protocol to help manage her urgent broadcasts more effectively.

> **Claire:** "Hey Amina, do you have a moment to talk about the last emergency meeting?"
>
> **Amina:** (*sighing*) "Claire, I know you couldn't make it, but we really needed everyone on that call. It was critical."
>
> **Claire:** "I understand, and I appreciate the urgency. Emergencies are inevitable, but I think we can manage them more effectively. Can we talk about establishing a simple protocol to handle these situations better?"
>
> **Amina:** "What do you mean? We already have a process. I call a meeting, and we sort it out."
>
> **Claire:** "I get that. But I think we can streamline it. What if we set up an emergency Slack channel? We can pin a RACI matrix there

so everyone knows who's responsible and accountable for different areas. This way, when an emergency arises, you can target the right people immediately."

Amina:

"I don't know, Claire. I'm used to just talking things out with everyone at once. It feels more efficient."

Claire: "It might seem that way, but dragging everyone into a call at odd hours can be really disruptive. It impacts work–life balance and team morale. By using a dedicated Slack channel, you can still get fast responses but in a more focused manner. The right people can jump in and take action, and the rest of the team can stay informed without being pulled away from their tasks."

Amina: (*hesitant*) "I'm not sure. What if something urgent comes up and the right person isn't available?"

Claire: "That's where the RACI matrix helps. It outlines who's responsible for what, and we can rotate on-call duties to ensure there's always someone available. Plus, this method still allows everyone to see the situation and pitch in if needed. It's about targeting the right people while keeping the team in the loop."

Amina: "It sounds good in theory, but I'm worried about the execution. What if it doesn't work?"

Claire: "We can start small and adjust as needed. I can help set it up and walk you through it. This approach will not only reduce the chaos during emergencies but also give you the best and fastest response. It's more efficient and less disruptive."

Amina: (*considering*) "Okay, we can try it. But I'll need your help to make sure it works smoothly."

Claire: "Absolutely. I'll get everything set up, and we can have a quick training session with the team. Let's aim to reduce those emergency broadcasts and handle crises more calmly and efficiently."

By implementing a structured emergency management protocol, Claire helps Amina understand the benefits of a more organized approach to crises. This method not only reduces the disruption caused by sudden emergency meetings but also ensures that the right people are involved quickly and effectively. Prevention and anticipation are key strategies in managing many managerial archetypes, including the Emergency Broadcaster.

Encourage Independent Research

Fostering a culture of self-sufficiency in your Emergency Broadcaster manager involves guiding them to conduct their own research before sounding the alarm and initiating an emergency broadcast. This proactive approach can significantly reduce the disruptive impact of last-minute crises by ensuring that your manager has the necessary information to make informed decisions without immediately resorting to calling everyone to action. Educating your manager isn't always welcome, easy, or retained, but using gentle suggestions and demonstrating the desired behavior are effective ways to manage upward.

- **Inbox Management:** Using effective search techniques and flagging and organizing information can help The Emergency Broadcaster manager create a repository of information that they can quickly navigate when a crisis does arise. If you're successful in helping them arrest their immediate instinct to ring the fire alarm, the hope is that they can turn to their inbox (or information hub equivalent) to gather details on the emergency and catch up quickly on the relevant communications and state of the situation before engaging with the team.
- **Effective Search Techniques:** Begin by gently suggesting or more effectively demonstrating how to manage their inbox effectively. Demonstrate how to use search functions to filter through emails and quickly find critical information. Show them how to use keywords, date ranges, and specific sender filters to streamline this process. For instance, you might say, "I've found that using specific keywords in the search bar helps me locate past emails quickly. It's been a game-changer for me when I need to reference previous communications."
- **Flagging and Organizing:** Encourage your manager to flag important emails and create folders for different projects or

topics. Demonstrate this by organizing your own emails and sharing how it has helped you stay on top of essential information. For example, "I started flagging critical emails and categorizing them into folders. It's helped me keep track of important updates and follow-ups. Maybe this could work for you too?"

Tools and Resources: Utilizing key tools and resources will help your manager conduct next level research where the information in their inboxes might be scattered and incomplete. Helping them quickly become familiar with and rely on organizational tools to deliver key information can help them find details to quell the emergency broadcast and even give them critical information to help guide their interactions with the team with reduced disruption.

Training on Tools: Offer to guide your manager through the various tools and resources available within the organization, such as project management software (Trello, Asana, Microsoft Teams), shared drives, wikis, and internal databases. Note that depending on your leader's technical proficiency, executive position within the organization, this might mean making it as simple as possible to interact with the tool. Many executives will rightly bristle if they have to dive into a project management tool to disposition an emergency, so make it easy for them. Provide gentle, ongoing support rather than one-time training. For instance, "I've been using Asana to keep track of our project milestones. I can show you how I use it to stay updated if you'd like."

Creating Checklists and FAQs: Develop checklists and FAQs that your manager can refer to when they sense an emerging issue. Share how these resources have benefited you. For example, "I put together a checklist for common issues and their solutions. It's been really helpful for troubleshooting before escalating problems. I can share it with you if you're interested."

Encouraging Specific Questions: Guide your manager to ask specific, targeted questions that can help them quickly assess situations. Demonstrate this in meetings by asking sharp questions yourself. For instance, instead of broadly asking,

"What's happening with Project X?" you might say, "Has the latest update on Project X been implemented, and what are the current roadblocks?"

Putting It Into Practice

Claire is working in her office when Amina drops by in a panic. A new demand has come from her boss, Haruto, and she needs to find out who is on point for delivering the project milestone review tomorrow. She's lost the Slack channel Claire set up and is about to resort to her old habit of broadcasting an emergency all-hands-on-deck meeting.

> **Amina:** (*frantic*) "Claire, Haruto just dumped this new demand on me, and I need to find out who's responsible for the project milestone review tomorrow. I can't find the Slack channel you set up. I think I need to call an emergency meeting to get to the bottom of this."
>
> **Claire:** "That does sound important. But before we toss a bomb into everyone's schedule, maybe I can help you find the information you need. I'm sure you already have everything in your inbox."
>
> **Amina:** (*impatient*) "I don't have time to climb through emails Claire. Haruto needs the update now."
>
> **Claire:** "I get it, but calling an emergency meeting will disrupt everyone's work. Give me five minutes to help you find the information first. I'll come to your office and show you how to search for it quickly."
>
> **Amina:** (*reluctant*) "Fine. Let's make it quick."
>
> **Claire:** (*in Amina's office*) "Alright, let's start by searching your inbox. Use the search bar and type in 'project milestone review.' Make sure to set the date range to the past month to narrow it down."
>
> **Amina:** (*typing*) "Okay, I see some emails. But there are so many of them."
>
> **Claire:** "Look for the email threads from our project management tool or any recent updates. You can also filter by sender to find emails from key team members involved in the project."

Amina: (*scrolling through emails*) "Here it is. I found an email from John detailing the project milestone review. It looks like he's on point for tomorrow."

Claire: "Perfect. See, you had the information all along. This is much better than pulling everyone into a meeting. By using your inbox effectively, you can save time and avoid unnecessary disruptions."

Amina: (*begrudgingly*) "I guess you're right. It just feels faster to talk it out sometimes."

Claire: "I understand, but this way, you target the right person directly. Plus, everyone else can stay focused on their tasks. It's all about finding the balance and using the tools we have effectively."

Amina: "Alright, I'll try to remember this next time. But you might have to remind me again."

Claire: "That's okay. We'll keep working on it. I'll make sure the Slack channel is pinned and easily accessible. Let's use these tools to our advantage and make our work smoother."

This type of management coping strategy—encouraging independent research and utilizing existing tools—is crucial in managing the Emergency Broadcaster. By helping your manager navigate their resources effectively, you can prevent unnecessary disruptions and foster a more efficient work environment. Prevention and anticipation are key strategies in managing many managerial archetypes, including the Emergency Broadcaster.

Summing It Up

Managing the Emergency Broadcaster archetype involves a blend of proactive planning, setting clear boundaries, and fostering independent research to prevent the frequent, disruptive emergency broadcasts that derail team productivity. The key to navigating this archetype lies in anticipation and prevention. By implementing specific coping strategies, you can help your manager stay informed and prepared, reducing the need for last-minute crises. Here are the key coping strategies:

1. **Set Clear Boundaries**: Clearly communicate your availability for meetings and urgent communications to balance professional responsibilities and personal well-being. Consistent enforcement of these boundaries helps maintain productivity and work–life balance. While you might face challenges, such as missing vital information, framing the conversation around mutual benefits can lead to better outcomes.

2. **Prevent Forest Fires**: Proactive planning and regular check-ins are crucial. Schedule short, focused meetings during quieter periods to review upcoming projects, milestones, and key meetings. Use these sessions to ensure that your manager is aware of potential trouble spots and can address them proactively. Follow up with detailed documentation and utilize technology like shared calendars and project management tools to keep information easily accessible and up to date.

3. **Establish an Emergency Protocol**: Develop a structured approach for handling crises, including a checklist of steps, key contacts, and resources. Create a list of team leaders and their responsibilities to streamline communication during emergencies. Set up dedicated communication channels, such as a specific Slack channel, and pin a RACI matrix to help funnel the manager to the right accountable parties. Guide responsible personnel to ask targeted questions to quickly gather necessary information.

4. **Encourage Independent Research**: Foster a culture of self-sufficiency by guiding your manager to conduct their own research before initiating an emergency broadcast. Demonstrate effective inbox management techniques and the use of organizational tools such as project management software and shared collaboration spaces. Provide ongoing support and create checklists and FAQs to help your manager quickly assess situations and find the necessary information.

Empathy plays a critical role in managing upward effectively. By understanding the pressures and motivations behind the Emergency Broadcaster's behavior, you can better communicate and implement strategies that foster a more balanced and strategic approach to crisis management. Encouraging your manager to conduct their own research and use existing tools can significantly reduce the frequency of emergency broadcasts, allowing the team to maintain a healthier work–life balance and higher morale.

The Emergency Broadcaster's reactive nature can be challenging, but with the right strategies in place, you can transform this high-stress management style into a more controlled and strategic leadership approach. By implementing these coping strategies and continually fostering a culture of proactive planning and independent research, you can help your manager lead more effectively and create a more stable and productive work environment for everyone.

CHAPTER 3

The Complainer

Background

Diego sat rigidly at the head of the polished conference table, his palms sweating as he awaited the arrival of Haruto, the new executive vice president renowned across several multinational organizations as a turnaround executive. Today was the day he would evaluate his division—a division of over a thousand people whose outputs, personnel, and budget he had tirelessly managed. The weight of uncertainty was palpable in the air, as his team of vice presidents shared nervous glances, each harboring their fears and speculations about the impending scrutiny.

As Haruto entered the room, his presence commanded immediate attention. Tall and imposing, with a reputation that preceded him, he greeted Diego and his team with a polite nod, his demeanor professional yet distant. Diego introduced his vice presidents, each of whom began presenting their scope of work, strategies, goals, and achievements. But as they delved into details, Haruto's incisive questions cut through their narratives. "What are the numbers backing this strategy?" he would ask, or "How do these outputs align with our OKRs?" Some of the questions stumped his team; they were not prepared for this level of scrutiny, and gaps in their metrics and OKRs were laid bare.

Diego's heart sank with every question Haruto posed that his team couldn't answer confidently. His fears about his grasp on the division were materializing before his eyes. The meeting, meant to be a show-case of his team's hard work, turned into a glaring exposure of over-looked metrics and unmet objectives. He felt exposed, his leadership questioned, his team's shortcomings unveiled for Haruto's critical eye. To make matters worse, many of the shortcomings were things that his own vice presidents had called out as areas of exposure, and he had ignored them or deprioritized them.

In the weeks that followed, Diego noticed a stark change in Haruto's engagement with the division. He devoted considerable time to his colleagues, who had strategic visions broken down into tactical programs, run by their vice presidents and backed by the right metrics. These were metrics that resonated with Haruto, metrics that Diego's division struggled to produce. Haruto's lack of interaction with him became a sore point. He found himself excluded from discussions that once would have sought his input.

This exclusion began to color Diego's view of his role and Haruto's intentions. In team meetings and division calls, his once optimistic and proactive demeanor gave way to negativity. "Haruto never talks to me," he would lament, or "He's continuously comparing me to the other managing vice presidents, implying he doesn't value what we do here." His words, tinged with bitterness and defeat, began to seep into the morale of his vice presidents and, by extension, the entire division.

The ripple effect of Diego's growing negativity was profound. His team, once buoyed by his leadership, now navigated their tasks with a sense of futility. The vision and enthusiasm that had characterized their efforts waned, replaced by a pervasive sense of being overlooked and undervalued. The division that had once thrived under Diego's guidance was now shadowed by doubt, its members grappling with the realization that their leader had succumbed to the poison of despair. The well of motivation and collaboration was tainted, leaving the once cohesive team fragmented and disheartened.

As Diego struggled with his perception of Haruto's indifference, the division's productivity and innovative spirit suffered. The once vibrant team meetings turned into sessions of commiseration, where the focus shifted from achievement and growth to grievances and dissatisfaction. Diego's inability to rise above his circumstances and lead with positivity not only compromised his leadership but also the very fabric of the division he was entrusted to guide.

The Archetype Defined

In the tapestry of managerial archetypes, The Complainer emerges as a figure steeped in dissatisfaction and vocal grievances. This manager navigates the corridors of their responsibilities with a cloud of discontent, their conversations saturated with critiques of upper management decisions, organizational policies, or the perennial hurdles that their team faces. It's a persona that seems more attuned to the art of lamentation than to leadership, focusing energy on highlighting problems rather than forging solutions.

For those who have worked under the shadow of The Complainer, the experience is both draining and disheartening. Meetings that could be platforms for collaborative problem-solving instead become stages for airing grievances. The Complainer's relentless focus on the negative aspects of work can sap the enthusiasm and innovation from their team, leaving individuals feeling helpless and demoralized. It creates an environment where cynicism breeds and morale dwindles, as the narrative of insurmountable challenges overshadows any sense of achievement or progress.

Have you ever found yourself in a meeting, the agenda set for progress updates and strategic discussions, only to hear your manager veer off course with remarks that echo a familiar refrain of dissatisfaction? The Complainer is a managerial archetype characterized by a penchant for vocalizing grievances, often exhibits behaviors that can turn even the most routine meetings into sessions of despair. Here are some common behaviors and phrases you might recognize:

During a project update meeting with direct reports:

"Once again, upper management has set unrealistic goals without understanding our challenges. It's like they're setting us up to fail."

"I don't even know why we bother with these initiatives if resources are always going to be pulled from under us at the last minute."

In a divisionwide meeting aimed at reviewing quarterly achievements:

"You know how it works here. … Other departments get all the recognition and resources. It's never a level playing field."

"I've raised our concerns to the higher-ups multiple times, but you can imagine how that went. It's like talking to a wall. They just don't listen or care."

When discussing future strategies or projects:

"Let's be real, no matter how much we plan, something always gets in the way. It's exhausting trying to innovate in this environment. This is why we are shifting our focus away from innovation."

"Why even propose new ideas? Every time we do, there's some excuse about budget constraints or shifting priorities."

During one-on-one sessions with team members:

"You're doing great work, but don't expect much to come of it. In this division, recognition is about who you know and how visible you are, not just what you do."

"I'd like to push for that promotion you deserve, but between you and me, it's probably not going to happen. The decision-makers have their favorites, and during performance calibration, where you're compared against your peers, only the popular managers come out on top."

These expressions of frustration, while perhaps grounded in genuine challenges, often overshadow the manager's role as a leader and motivator. Instead of fostering a culture of problem-solving and resilience, The Complainer inadvertently cultivates an atmosphere of cynicism and stagnation. Recognizing these patterns is the first step toward navigating and ultimately transcending the limitations imposed by such a managerial style.

Research shows that negative leadership behaviors, such as constant complaining, can significantly lower team morale and increase employee turnover.[*] When managers continuously focus on negatives and voice their frustrations without offering solutions, it creates a toxic work environment. This negativity can demoralize employees, making them feel undervalued and unappreciated. Over time, this leads to disengagement, decreased productivity, and ultimately, higher turnover rates as employees seek more positive and supportive work environments.

Yet, within the echoes of The Complainer's grievances lies a cry for help—a signal that, beneath the surface, there might be a leader struggling with feelings of inadequacy or isolation. Their constant complaints may be a misguided attempt at connection, seeking validation or support from their team in the only way they know how. This understanding doesn't excuse the behavior but offers a pathway to empathy and perhaps, a bridge to constructive change.

Core Analysis

At the heart of The Complainer archetype lies a spiraling storm, a hurricane of negative energy that feeds and grows from its own despair. This tempest is neither sudden nor abrupt but builds gradually, each layer of criticism and dissatisfaction adding fuel to its core, driving the winds of discontent to gale-force speeds. The Complainer finds themselves in the eye of this storm, a place where the calm belies the chaos encircling them, unaware that they are both the creator and the prisoner of this turbulent environment.

The genesis of this storm often lies in genuine challenges and setbacks, yet it's the response to these difficulties that distinguishes The Complainer from other leaders. Instead of seeking solutions or adapting strategies, they fixate on the obstacles, amplifying them through constant vocalization. This focus on the negative becomes a

[*]Journal of Business Ethics (2017). The Effects of Negative Leadership on Employee Outcomes. Journal of Business Ethics. Retrieved from Journal of Business Ethics.

self-perpetuating cycle; each complaint reinforces their jaded perspective, making the storm's eye—where they reside—seem like the only place of truth. It's a state of mind that becomes a prison, one whose bars are invisible to them, constructed from years of accumulated grievances and perceived injustices.

In this prison of their own making, The Complainer fails to realize the impact of their words and attitude on those around them. Their relentless negativity acts as a repellent, pushing away opportunities for growth and collaboration. Team members, initially empathetic, find themselves gradually worn down by the constant barrage of pessimism. Studies highlight how managers who constantly complain can reduce employee engagement and motivation, leading to decreased productivity.[†] The atmosphere becomes toxic, stifling innovation and enthusiasm under the heavy cloud of the leader's discontent.

As this environment deteriorates, team members may begin to seek escape, leaving in search of more positive climates. Each departure reinforces The Complainer's belief in their narrative of defeat and isolation, further intensifying the storm. It's a self-fulfilling prophecy; they view each resignation not as a consequence of their actions but as validation of their grievances against the organization or the world at large. Unwittingly, The Complainer perpetuates a cycle of negativity that validates their jaded view, yet each confirmation of their bleak outlook only tightens the chains of their imprisonment.

This invisible prison is particularly insidious because The Complainer often doesn't recognize they're confined within it. They perceive themselves as merely realistic, the lone voice willing to acknowledge the harsh truths of their environment. However, this mindset traps them in a cycle from which escape seems impossible, not because the doors are locked, but because they've forgotten how to see them, let alone seek them out. Breaking free requires a monumental shift in perspective, a willingness to challenge the storm's power by acknowledging their role in its creation and taking the first steps toward seeking the sun beyond the clouds.

[†]Ibid.

Understanding the motivation behind The Complainer archetype is crucial for professionals navigating the challenging waters of working under such a boss. Recognizing that this behavior often stems from a complex mix of past disappointments, perceived injustices, and perhaps a sense of isolation or undervaluation can transform how one perceives and reacts to their negativity. This insight offers a strategic advantage—it equips you with the empathy to see beyond the surface-level frustrations, enabling a more compassionate and effective approach to communication and collaboration. By comprehending the underlying causes of your boss's complaints, you can better navigate conversations, deftly steering them toward more positive and productive outcomes. Furthermore, this understanding can help prevent the contagion of negativity, allowing you to maintain your morale and motivation. Essentially, grasping the motivations of The Complainer not only aids in building a more harmonious working relationship but also serves as a vital shield for your professional well-being and career progression.

Coping Strategies

Some Complainers seem to have a natural predisposition toward negativity, perhaps as a deeply ingrained aspect of their personality or a learned behavior from early life or professional experiences. However, many find themselves adopting this outlook after experiencing stinging defeats or setbacks, often following a series of successful achievements. The contrast between past victories and present frustrations can be particularly disheartening, leading previously optimistic individuals into a spiral of continuous complaining. It's crucial, therefore, to safeguard against becoming a complainer by cultivating resilience, seeking out positive perspectives, and engaging in reflective practices that help maintain a balanced outlook on professional challenges. Recognizing the potential for this transformation is the first step in ensuring that setbacks do not irrevocably alter one's approach to challenges and interactions in the workplace.

Use Empathy to Build a Road to Action

The key to coexisting with The Complainer begins with empathy—understanding the storms they've weathered that led them to where they are. This understanding doesn't mean condoning endless negativity but rather recognizing it as a cry for help or a sign of deeper issues. However, empathy must be balanced with the establishment of positive boundaries to protect your own mental and emotional well-being. It's essential to learn the art of listening without absorbing the negativity, maintaining an equilibrium where your own positivity isn't drowned out by their storm.

Putting It Into Practice

In a softly lit corner of the office, Marcus approaches Diego, who's visibly agitated after a particularly challenging meeting with upper management.

> **Marcus**: "Diego, I can see you're really frustrated with how things went today. It's tough when it feels like our efforts aren't being recognized. I'm here to support you and the team through this."
>
> **Diego:** "It's like no matter what we do, it's never enough for them. I'm at my wit's end, Marcus. I just don't know what they expect from us anymore."
>
> **Marcus:** "I understand where you're coming from, and it's valid to feel this way. What if we focus on what we can control and work on a plan together? We've overcome challenges before, and I'm confident we can do it again. How about we set some time to outline our strategy and document our progress? It might give us a clearer perspective and something positive to present."

In this brief exchange, Marcus validates Diego's feelings, demonstrating empathy toward his situation, yet subtly steers the conversation toward a constructive outcome. By suggesting a focus on actionable steps and documentation, Marcus introduces a positive boundary to channel Diego's frustrations into productive planning, showcasing a balanced approach to dealing with The Complainer.

Use Solution-Focused Engagement and Documentation

When confronted with a barrage of complaints, following a period of honest empathy and seeking to understand The Complainer's emotional state, steering the conversation toward solutions can be a beacon of light. It shifts the focus from problems to possibilities, marking you as a lighthouse amidst the fog of grievances. Concurrently, keeping a detailed log of successes and setbacks serves as a tangible reminder of progress and effort, valuable during discussions to gently remind The Complainer of the team's achievements and resilience. This dual approach of focusing on solutions while documenting the journey encourages a more objective view of the situation, helping to dissipate some of the clouds of negativity.

Putting It Into Practice

After a department meeting where Diego voiced numerous concerns about project delays and budget cuts, Marcus finds a moment to engage with him, aiming to pivot toward a more solution-oriented dialogue.

> **Marcus**: "Diego, I share your concerns about the delays and the budget issues. I was thinking. … Could we explore some creative solutions together? Perhaps there are alternative strategies we haven't considered yet."
>
> **Diego:** "I just don't see a way forward, Marcus. Every direction seems blocked. And even if we find a workaround, how do we keep track of everything without getting overwhelmed?"
>
> **Marcus:** "That's a valid point. What if we start documenting our brainstorming sessions and the outcomes? Not only could this help us track our progress and refine our strategies, but it would also allow us to present a clear plan to upper management.
> It might just be the structured approach we need to navigate through these obstacles. Let me take the first step and I'll organize a framework we can all follow."

In this interaction, Marcus acknowledges Diego's frustrations, aligning with his perspective to establish a common ground. He then gently shifts the focus toward identifying potential solutions, suggesting a methodical approach to documentation as a tool for clarity and accountability. Finally, he takes the initiative to put the recommended practice into motion. This solution-focused engagement aims to transform challenges into opportunities for strategic planning and positive action. And volunteering to take the first step indicates to The Complainer manager that they are not alone and that you are committed to taking a positive approach to addressing what seems like a jaded negative cloud hovering over them.

Cultivating Positivity and Professional Development

Cultivating positivity is crucial when dealing with The Complainer manager archetype. Start by building a support network among colleagues who maintain a constructive outlook. Actively contribute to a culture that celebrates every achievement, no matter how small. Regularly recognize team achievements and milestones, creating an atmosphere of positivity that can counterbalance the negativity from The Complainer. This recognition not only boosts team morale but can also help The Complainer see the positive impact of their team's efforts.

Engage in regular reflection to assess and improve your strategies for handling negativity. For example, consider implementing "wins of the week" sessions where the team shares successes and progress. Also consider encouraging (formal or informal) professional development opportunities for yourself, your team members, and even The Complainer manager. The investment of professional development time and activities can signify to the team that they are indeed important and is essentially a vote of confidence in them extended by their manager and the organization. This can reinvigorate the team with a new sense of possibility and have a contagious positive effect, traveling upstream to The Complainer manager themselves. Investing in personnel (yourself included) opens up new avenues and can help chip away at the negative spiral fostered by The Complainer. By fostering a positive atmosphere and recognizing achievements, you can help mitigate the effects of The Complainer and promote a more balanced, constructive work environment.

Keep in mind however that despite these efforts, in some rare instances, no matter how much cheerleading and recognition happen, the negative shadow may be too entrenched, despite your best efforts. If the situation becomes too overwhelming, seek external perspectives through mentorship or professional advice for new strategies in managing difficult interactions. Ultimately, if your current role stifles your growth with constant complaints, it may be time to seek a more positive and supportive environment that aligns with your long-term career goals.

Putting It Into Practice

Following a particularly negative team meeting where Diego lamented over recent department failures, Marcus catches up with him in his office, hoping to inject a sense of positivity and focus on growth.

> **Marcus:** "Diego, I've noticed the team seems really disheartened lately. I was thinking, what if we start recognizing small wins in our meetings? Celebrating progress can really lift everyone's spirits and shift our focus."
>
> **Diego:** "It feels like there's not much to celebrate, Marcus. Everything's just been … tough. And honestly, I'm not sure if focusing on the small stuff will make any difference."
>
> **Marcus:** "I understand it seems daunting, but fostering a positive atmosphere might change our perspective and help us see solutions we've overlooked. Plus, focusing on professional development could reenergize the team. Maybe we could look into workshops or training sessions that align with our goals. It's about growth, for us and the team. What if I do the work to put together a set of goal-based training that we can evaluate together as a team as a first step?"

In this conversation, Marcus attempts to subtly shift Diego's focus from the pervasive negativity to cultivating a more positive, growth-oriented mindset. By suggesting the acknowledgment of small victories and investing in professional development, Marcus introduces a strategy aimed at building resilience and fostering a supportive environment that encourages continuous learning and improvement. The key thing he also does well is that he once again takes the initiative and breaks the complex challenge into a small, addressable next step.

Navigating the tempestuous waters surrounding The Complainer requires a compass of empathy, the anchor of positive boundaries, and the sails of solution-focused engagement. By charting a course that values personal well-being and professional growth, you can not only survive the storm but also emerge with newfound strength and resilience, ready to navigate even the choppiest of waters.

Summing It Up

In the shadow of The Complainer, professionals find themselves navigating a landscape marked by storms of grievances and showers of dissatisfaction. Yet, within this environment, there are pathways to clearer skies, strategies that not only help manage the downpour but can also transform the climate into one of growth and positivity. Here's how to weather the storm and emerge stronger:

1. **Empathize and Establish Boundaries:** Begin with understanding the root of the complaints, which often lie in past frustrations or a feeling of being undervalued. Approach The Complainer with empathy to validate their feelings. Simultaneously, protect your positivity and work–life balance by establishing emotional and schedule boundaries that prevent you from being pulled into the vortex of negativity.

2. **Shift Toward Solutions and Documentation:** Steer conversations away from endless problem discussions toward actionable solutions. Encourage The Complainer to focus on what can be done rather than what can't. Coupled with diligent documentation, this strategy ensures that every challenge is met with a proactive plan, turning potential complaints into opportunities for improvement and success.

3. **Cultivate Positivity and Professional Growth:** Introduce a culture of recognition within your team or division, celebrat-

ing even the smallest wins to counterbalance the negativity. Promote professional development opportunities, encouraging The Complainer and the team to focus on growth and learning. This fosters an environment where progress is acknowledged and valued, diluting the impact of complaints.

4. **Engage in Constructive Conversations:** Initiate open and honest dialogues that aim to address and mitigate the core issues behind the complaints. Use "Talk It Out" sessions as a tool to break down barriers, offering a platform where concerns can be expressed and addressed in a constructive manner. This approach helps in building a bridge over the turbulent waters, leading toward mutual understanding and respect.

Implementing these strategies requires patience, persistence, and a deep commitment to positive change. By empathizing, focusing on solutions, fostering a positive environment, and engaging in constructive conversations, you can navigate the challenging terrain of The Complainer. This journey not only transforms your professional relationship with such a manager but also empowers you to cultivate a resilient and positive mindset, capable of thriving in any environment. Start practicing these strategies tomorrow and watch as the landscape around The Complainer gradually shifts toward a more productive and harmonious space.

CHAPTER 4

The Amnesiac

Background

In the bustling ecosystem of the organization, Rajesh found himself at the helm of a project poised to redefine the landscape of their industry. It was a transformative initiative, threading through the complex web of stakeholders, engineering teams, and external consulting firms. The project promised to demystify groundbreaking technologies, paving the way for new business models and untapped revenue streams. Rajesh, aware of the monumental scope, had meticulously rallied consensus, weaving together the disparate threads of support into a cohesive tapestry of commitment and enthusiasm.

At the core of this intricate network was Emily, whose political sway and budgetary approval were crucial. After numerous meetings, presentations, and discussions, Rajesh had secured her written and verbal consent, a green light that set the wheels of progress in motion. Or so he thought.

During a routine standup, with the blueprint of their future laid out before them, Emily's question cut through the room like a cold gust of wind.

"Why are we doing this project again? What's the true value here, and who agreed to this?"

The room fell into a stunned silence. Rajesh's mind raced, confusion and frustration mounting as he tried to reconcile Emily's sudden amnesia with the clear approvals she had given just weeks prior. As Rajesh scrambled to remind her of the discussions, the approvals, and the shared vision they had articulated, Emily seemed to drift further away, her questions now laced with skepticism. She began to relitigate the project's merits, picking apart its value and questioning its necessity, as if hearing about it for the first time. Rajesh's agitation grew, his efforts to steer Emily back to their agreed-upon course grew increasingly futile.

Finally, Emily's words fell like a hammer, "Let's put this project on hold for now."

The decision was as inexplicable to Rajesh as it was to the rest of the team, all of whom had witnessed the project's potential and Emily's previous support. The collective dismay was palpable, a shared disbelief at the unraveling of what had promised to be a game-changing initiative. Rajesh was left grappling with the fallout, the project's momentum halted by the very person who had once championed it. The frustration and confusion within the team were mirrored in the broader organization, where the news of the project's suspension spread like ripples, reaching the stakeholders and external partners who had invested their trust and resources.

This sudden shift, driven by Emily's forgetfulness, not only stalled a transformative project but also cast a shadow of doubt over the leadership's coherence and the organization's capacity for innovation. Rajesh found himself at a crossroads, reflecting on the challenges of navigating leadership amnesia, and contemplating strategies to safeguard future initiatives from similar fates. The task ahead was clear: to reconstruct the bridge of understanding and commitment, piece by piece, in the hope of resurrecting the project and steering it back to its visionary course.

The Archetype Defined

Within the dynamic ecosystem of workplace archetypes, The Amnesiac emerges as a particularly perplexing character, navigating the professional landscape with a memory as fleeting as shadows at dusk. This archetype isn't defined by a lack of interest or engagement but rather by an elusive grasp on past discussions, decisions, and commitments. Like a boat adrift in a vast ocean without an anchor, The Amnesiac often finds themselves revisiting the same ports of conversation, unaware they've charted these waters before.

The presence of The Amnesiac in leadership positions introduces a unique set of challenges and frustrations, transforming the task of project advancement into a Sisyphean ordeal. Teams under their guidance frequently experience déjà vu, meticulously laying the groundwork for initiatives, securing approvals, and celebrating milestones, only to find these achievements vanish in the fog of their leader's forgetfulness. What was once a clear directive becomes a question mark, with projects and strategies subjected to constant reevaluation and justification, as if being considered for the first time.

This cycle is not born out of malice or disinterest; rather, it often stems from an overwhelming influx of information, competing priorities, or perhaps a disconnect from the intricate details of every project under their purview. Research highlights that managerial forgetfulness can stem from cognitive overload and impacts team efficiency by causing repeated tasks and miscommunications.[*] The Amnesiac manager creates a confusing and stressful environment where progress is paradoxically both constant and stagnant, a realm where forward motion is perpetually interrupted by the need to retrace steps and reaffirm commitments.

Despite the arsenal of strategies and coping mechanisms previously outlined to navigate the challenges posed by other manager archetypes, it's crucial to acknowledge that these approaches are not infallible, especially when dealing with The Amnesiac. The very nature of this manager archetype, marked by a chronic forgetfulness and an overwhelming influx of responsibilities, can render even the most meticulous paper trails and recorded testimonies ineffective. Surprisingly, this archetype, when confronted with documentation that contradicts their current understanding or exposes their forgetfulness, may not only fail to recognize or recall these commitments but they may also react defensively to the existence of such evidence.

The combination of their embarrassment over not remembering key details, which everyone else seems to recall vividly, and the frustration of being presented with incontrovertible data affirming their prior agreements, can lead to rash and emotionally charged decisions. These

---

[*]Journal of Management Studies, 2016, "The Impact of Cognitive Overload on Managerial Performance," https://onlinelibrary.wiley.com/doi/10.1111/joms.12120.

impulsive reactions, born out of a mix of denial and wounded pride, can exacerbate tensions within teams and, in more severe cases, result in decisions that inadvertently undermine project progress and harm the organizational climate. In this context, navigating The Amnesiac's waters requires not just strategic documentation and communication but also a nuanced understanding of human motivations and the patience to manage the delicate balance between reminding and reengaging.

Core Analysis

All busy managers, including professionals across various fields, operate with what can be likened to a computer's RAM stack—a high-performance, short-term memory cache that holds the most relevant and immediately necessary information for quick access. Analogous to this is the concept of ROM, representing long-term memory storage, where larger projects, comprehensive roadmaps, and overarching strategies are kept for sustained tactical efforts. Effective leadership requires a seamless interplay between these two types of memory: RAM for the agility to respond to immediate needs and ROM for the continuity and consistency of long-term objectives. However, The Amnesiac archetype often struggles with efficiently transitioning crucial information from RAM to ROM, necessitating aids and strategies to bridge this gap. In contrast, more mature managers have honed the skill of not just retaining but also categorizing and retrieving information from both types of memory with ease, ensuring their leadership remains both responsive and visionary.

The Amnesiac archetype, therefore, embodies a challenge of communication and documentation. If you asked any manager if they want to be this way, they would likely say no, or even perhaps deny exhibiting this behavior altogether. They are often overleveraged, overwhelmed, and dealing with too many things simultaneously to ever reflect, commit things to memory, and take a longer strategic view. Constantly in short-term resolution mode, these managers are typically juggling too many direct reports, management demands, and overall demands on their time. It's a testament to the critical importance of clear, concise, and repetitive information sharing and the establishment of robust systems for tracking decisions and actions. Navigating the complexities of working with The Amnesiac requires empathy, patience, structured communication strategies, and an unyielding commitment to clarity and record-keeping, transforming the ephemeral into the enduring.

Coping Strategies

It may seem inconceivable that when talking to a manager who embodies the behaviors associated with The Amnesiac archetype, that they will most likely agree with your plans and approaches to addressing work in the short term but seemingly execute a 180° turn around the next time you talk with them. Eventually and inevitably, they will deconstruct the road you've carefully planned as if the conversation, documentation, and support never happened. The feeling of stark disbelief you may experience the first few times this happens is upsetting and jarring.

However, to cope with this pattern of behavior, you must learn to anticipate it in a very similar way to The Surprised manager archetype. By beginning to learn and assume that they will forget, you'll sidestep the shock and horror that comes with The Amnesiac pulling the rug out from underneath you at critical and surprising points in your roadmap. Navigating the challenges posed by The Amnesiac manager requires a multifaceted approach, blending documentation, communication, empathy, and strategic reinforcement. Here's a comprehensive guide to managing this unique managerial archetype.

Practice a Unified Documentation and Communication Strategy

Crafting a robust coping strategy for working with The Amnesiac manager archetype involves creating a harmonious blend of enhanced documentation, strategic communication, and the use of visual aids because these tools help ensure that important information is consistently reinforced, easily accessible, and clearly understood, thereby reducing the frequency and impact of forgetfulness on team productivity and morale. If no amount of documentation will address this archetype's forgetfulness when it matters most, you might wonder why documentation is a coping strategy at all. This is a valid viewpoint, but the type of documentation you create when dealing with The Amnesiac must change. This documentation, and its frequent presentation to The Amnesiac manager (the unified approach), allows you to help manage your boss's transition of concepts from RAM to ROM.

> **Create Documentation Beacons:** When dealing with The Amnesiac manager archetype, traditional forms of documentation, no matter how meticulously maintained, may fall short in moments that matter most. The challenge isn't just about creating records but ensuring these records make a lasting impact on a memory that seems ever-ephemeral. In this context, the type of documentation required undergoes a transformation, leaning heavily on visual aids designed to act almost like mnemonic devices. These are not just reminders but beacons, crafted to keep critical concepts afloat in the manager's RAM stack (their working memory that they frequently use to make decisions in the moment) and to have them persisted to ROM. Without these aids, documentation and information slips from this immediate memory and evaporates, rarely solidifying into long-term recall, making it imperative to "pin" these concepts through specialized documentation. Short, powerful, and frequent visual cues—be it simple slides, charts, graphs, or graphics—are essential. These should be directly linked with key project themes, allowing The Amnesiac to visually and mentally connect with the information. This approach transcends traditional documentation, offering a lifeline to crucial data in a format that's not just seen but remembered.

> **Establish a Data Baseline:** Start by establishing a comprehensive system of documentation that meticulously records decisions, meetings, and key project milestones. This serves as your data baseline and helps when you need to create higher order conceptual visuals and documentation. Elevate this practice by integrating regular recaps and reminders into all forms of team

communication. At the start of each meeting, offer a brief recap of previously discussed topics, decisions made, and actions agreed upon to ensure that all team members, especially The Amnesiac, are on the same page. Remember that this documentation must include persistent key visuals and brief descriptions that remind your manager of the "why" behind the "what" to help them pin these concepts in their ephemeral RAM stack. The continuous presentation of these key visuals, including a consistent way of speaking and talking about the topic, will help keep the concepts pinned and help transition them into longer-term memory for the manager.

Employ Beacons and Straightforward Communication Together: Emphasize clear, structured communication in all interactions, using straightforward language and avoiding ambiguity. This approach ensures that crucial information is conveyed effectively and reduces the likelihood of misunderstandings or forgotten details. Complement these efforts with the strategic use of visual aids and summaries based on your meticulously crafted detailed data. Create charts, graphs, and bullet-point lists that highlight critical project components, timelines, and responsibilities. These visual tools serve as easily digestible reminders that can help anchor key points in the memory of The Amnesiac and facilitate quicker recall of important project details.

This unified strategy blends documentation and communication into a cohesive approach, providing a clear, organized framework that helps mitigate the challenges posed by The Amnesiac's tendency to forget. By employing these practices diligently, you create a supportive environment that not only aids in retaining essential information but also fosters a culture of clarity and accountability.

Putting It Into Practice

During a critical standup meeting, as the team gathers around, Emily's questioning gaze falls on Rajesh. The air is thick with anticipation;

Rajesh knows this moment is crucial for the future of their organization-wide transformative project.

> **Emily:** "Can someone remind me why we're prioritizing this project again? What's the true value here, and who exactly is on board with this?"

Rajesh, prepared for this moment, doesn't miss a beat. He had anticipated this, knowing Emily's tendency to forget key details. He quickly references a vivid visual aid he brought specifically for this purpose.

> **Rajesh:** "Absolutely, Emily. Let's look at this infographic."

Rajesh displays a colorful chart on the screen that he's shown Emily at least three times before. Note that he doesn't need to say that she's seen it already, thereby making her bristle at the subtle message that she hasn't been paying attention. Instead, he imagines what it is like to be her, potentially seeing something familiar, but in essence explaining to the slide like it's the first time she's seen it.

> **Rajesh:** "Here's the scope of the project, visually capturing its benefits. We're not just talking about incremental improvements; we're laying the groundwork for entirely new business models that tap into unexplored revenue streams."

He points to specific sections of the graphic, highlighting the strategic advantages and the broad spectrum of support from key stakeholders. He continues, indicating a timeline at the bottom of the infographic and includes a gentle, nonaccusatory reminder that not only she as well as others have already given Rajesh the green light.

> **Rajesh:** "And here, is when we last discussed this. You, along with the heads of each department, gave it the green light, recognizing its potential to position us as front-runners in the market."

Emily, peering at the infographic, nods slowly. The visual triggers a flicker of recognition.

> **Emily:** "Yes, I remember this conversation now. This was when we talked about leveraging a new set of cloud technologies, right?"

Rajesh: "Exactly! We discussed how these technologies could revolutionize our approach, offering us a competitive edge. Here are the key benefits we outlined"

Rajesh points to a section of the infographic that succinctly summarizes the project's advantages. Seeing Emily's growing understanding, he seizes the moment to reiterate the project's milestones and the next steps, ensuring she grasps the critical path forward.

Rajesh: "And with your continued support, we're on track to achieve these milestones."

Rajesh concludes by subtly using the phrase "continued support" to remind her that she's already seen this information and given her approval previously, affirming the project's trajectory.

Emily: "I see the bigger picture now. Thanks for jogging my memory, Rajesh. Let's ensure we keep these visuals handy for our updates. They really help focus our discussions."

Rajesh's quick thinking and strategic use of a visual aid not only averted potential deconstruction and sabotage of the project by The Amnesiac manager but also reinforced the project's significance and ensured alignment on its objectives, setting a precedent for future interactions.

Also note that he doesn't make her feel exposed or embarrassed that she doesn't remember. He simply retrieves evidence indicating when she, and a cohort of other project sponsors, agreed to provide their support for the project, thereby eliminating any unwanted emotions that would force Emily to react emotionally at her mental oversight.

Engage With Empathetic Persistence

Your instinct might be to think things like, "Forgetfulness just isn't acceptable at this level," or, "I can't jump through all these hoops just because you can't remember your responsibilities, commitments, or promises." While these thoughts stem from understandable frustrations, dwelling on them or letting them influence your interactions can inadvertently lead you down the path of becoming a Complainer yourself, trapped in a cycle of negativity that does little to improve the situation. The key to navigating this terrain lies not in assigning blame or harboring resentment but in strategically focusing on preserving your own projects and goals.

Understand Through Positive Empathy: If asked, I'm sure they don't mean to forget, nor is it preferable. Understanding this, apply a modicum of effort, as described, to implement supportive strategies such as empathetic engagement and structured communication. This approach allows you to accommodate and address the shortcomings in a constructive manner, ensuring the continuity of your agendas and roadmaps. It's about balancing understanding with efficiency, creating an environment where challenges are met with solutions rather than complaints. By doing so, you protect not only the progress of your projects but also foster a positive, collaborative atmosphere that elevates the entire team, including those who may struggle with forgetfulness.

- Navigating the challenges posed by working with The Amnesiac manager archetype calls for a nuanced approach that marries empathy with unwavering patience and persistence. Empathetic persistence in engagement revolves around understanding the underlying reasons behind a manager's forgetfulness, be it an overwhelming workload, stress, or a simple mismatch in their organizational skills. Approaching interactions with a foundation of empathy acknowledges these challenges and provides a supportive atmosphere conducive to positive outcomes.

Persistently Reinforce Key Messages: However, empathy alone might not suffice when faced with repetitive forgetfulness that risks project momentum and team morale. Herein lies the importance of patience and persistence—steadily reinforcing key messages, revisiting agreed-upon decisions, and patiently reiterating project details as necessary without showing frustration or annoyance. It's about maintaining a gentle, yet firm approach to communication, ensuring that crucial information remains at the forefront of discussions and decisions.

- Empathetic persistence in engagement involves strategically using reminders, visual aids, and documentation to aid memory, but doing so in a way that feels supportive rather than accusatory. It means acknowledging The Amnesiac's situation and working together to find effective methods to keep valuable information accessible and top of mind. This approach doesn't just aim to mitigate the effects of forgetfulness but seeks to build a stronger, more understanding working relationship, fostering a sense of teamwork and shared goals despite the challenges.

By combining empathy with patience and persistence, this strategy offers a respectful and effective way to enhance communication and project execution with The Amnesiac manager, ensuring that critical initiatives remain on track while also nurturing a positive and inclusive team environment.

Putting It Into Practice

After successfully navigating a potentially tumultuous staff meeting by refreshingly reminding Emily of crucial project details, Rajesh seeks a moment to connect with her privately, aiming to reinforce their working relationship with understanding and empathy.

Rajesh: "Emily, I'm glad we could go over the project details again during the meeting. I know how easy it can be for things to slip through the cracks, especially with the massive responsibilities you shoulder managing a division of over a thousand people."

Emily: "Thanks, Rajesh. I must admit, it's overwhelming at times. There's so much going on, and I appreciate your understanding. It's frustrating to forget important details, but it's a reality of the workload I'm dealing with."

Rajesh: "I completely understand, and I want you to know it's part of my job to help make it easier for you to keep track of the commitments related to our projects. Keeping you informed about the 'why,' the 'what,' and the 'how' is essential for our mutual success. It's important to me that the methods I'm using to remind you are helpful and not intrusive."

Emily: "Your approach today was spot-on. Having those visual aids and the succinct summary really helped jog my memory. It's a good system we have, but I'm open to any adjustments if you think there are more efficient ways to keep me updated."

Rajesh: "I'm glad to hear that worked for you. I'll continue to use visual summaries and concise points for our updates. And I'm always looking for ways to streamline our communication further, so if there's anything specific you'd like to change or try, just let me know."

In this dialogue, Rajesh applies the strategy of empathetic reinforcement, acknowledging the pressure and workload Emily faces while ensuring that his support is seen as a valuable asset rather than a burden. By opening the floor for feedback, Rajesh demonstrates his commitment to adaptability and collaboration, ensuring that their communication strategy remains effective and supportive. This conversation exemplifies how understanding paired with strategic action can transform potential points of contention into opportunities for strengthening teamwork and leadership support.

Adaptive Project Management With Feedback Loops

Integrating feedback loops with adaptive project management tools presents a strategic approach to mitigating the challenges posed by The Amnesiac manager, particularly during the critical initial stages of project proposals and development. This combined strategy is especially crucial as the nascent phases of initiatives are where The Amnesiac's forgetfulness can wreak the most havoc, potentially derailing projects before they gain momentum. A forgetful deconstruction following a positive commitment can not only frustrate project champions but can also seed doubt among other stakeholders, undermining their confidence and commitment.

Creating a safe and low-risk space for employees to probe and explore the degree to which The Amnesiac forgets about key projects, deliverables, and initiatives is essential. By utilizing a feedback loop early on, you can connect with your manager and examine in a low-risk environment the degree to which they forget. This approach is preferable to discovering these lapses by surprise in high-stakes meetings with team members or executive leadership. By preexploring, you can remind them before it really counts, utilizing empathy to speed the transition of key points to their ROM. Combined with a toolchain foundation that supports information delivery through reminders, visuals, and dashboards, this can be a method to head off any forgetful disruptions before they can do any lasting damage.

Establish a Safe Feedback Environment: Encourage a culture where feedback is shared openly and without fear of repercussions. Schedule regular check-ins where you can discuss ongoing projects and any concerns about memory lapses in a nonconfrontational manner. This helps in gauging the extent of forgetfulness in a controlled setting.

Utilize Adaptive Project Management Tools: Implement project management software that allows for regular updates and visual tracking of project milestones. Tools such as Trello, Asana, or Microsoft Teams can provide visual aids and reminders that reinforce memory. These tools help keep key information accessible and top of mind for The Amnesiac manager. Note that these tools must present the information to the manager. Don't expect the manager to proactively go into these tools and dig for the information.

Incorporate Visual and Repetitive Reminders: Use charts, graphs, and dashboards that can be frequently referenced to reinforce memory. Visual aids can act as mnemonic devices, helping to transition important information from short-term (RAM) to long-term memory (ROM). Ensure that these visuals are simple, direct, and consistently used in all communications.

Preemptive Reminders: Before critical meetings, send concise, visual summaries of key points that need to be remembered. This can include summaries of previous decisions, upcoming deadlines, and essential project details. These preemptive reminders ensure that your manager is well-prepared and reduces the likelihood of forgetful disruptions.

By implementing these strategies, you can effectively manage The Amnesiac manager's forgetfulness, ensuring that essential information is retained and recalled when needed. This proactive approach not only preserves project momentum but also fosters a more supportive and collaborative work environment.

Putting It Into Practice

Rajesh prepares for the monthly project update meeting, understanding the importance of delivering clear, concise updates on the project's progress. He's aware that a strong presentation will not only highlight the team's achievements but also positively showcase Emily, potentially mending her strained relationship with their executive leadership, including Haruto who will be in attendance at this update meeting.

As the meeting progresses, Rajesh confidently outlines the project's current status, emphasizing how strategic decisions have kept the initiative both under budget and on schedule. He is about to transition to discussing future phases when Emily interrupts with a question that sends a ripple of tension through the room.

Emily: "Wait, why are you accelerating in this sprint? Shouldn't we focus first on conducting more intense requirements reviews? We have to get this right. I don't recall agreeing to this approach. Shouldn't we reconsider moving ahead too quickly and how costly that might be?"

Rajesh recognizes the critical moment he's in. He's not flummoxed in this moment because he anticipated Emily's forgetfulness. He quickly accesses the project roadmap, a visual aid designed not only for clarity but also as a mnemonic device for The Amnesiac.

Rajesh: "Great question Emily, let me quickly refer us to the project roadmap we agreed upon."

Rajesh demonstrates his calm by using the phrase "great question" to indicate that he's prepared for this disruption, even though it's the opposite of a great question. He projects the roadmap on the screen, pointing to a specific decision point.

Rajesh: "Here's where we discussed this direction and agreed it was the best course of action, considering the benefits and the constraints we were operating under. This approach aligns with our overall strategy and objectives, which we all, including Haruto, supported during our last review."

Emily, momentarily pausing, looks at the visual roadmap. The visual cue sparks her memory, and she nods, a sign of recognition crossing her features.

Emily: "OK. I just want to make sure that we don't prematurely progress where there is any significant uncertainty."

Rajesh: "That's a sensible caution and we will definitely keep that in mind as we progress. In fact, in our next update, I'll make sure to bring this up so we can all have confidence that we're making progress in the right way."

Rajesh swiftly moves forward, reiterating the project's successes and how their collective decision-making has led to positive outcomes. He concludes the update by emphasizing the project's alignment with the organizational goals and its promising trajectory.

Haruto, who has been quietly observing, finally speaks up.

Haruto: "I'm happy with the progress and how well this team, under Rajesh and Emily's leadership, has navigated the challenges. Let's keep moving forward as planned."

The meeting concludes on a high note, with Rajesh successfully navigating a potentially disruptive moment through anticipating her forgetfulness around this point with preemptive feedback loops, employing quick thinking and the strategic use of coping mechanisms. His actions not only preserved the project's momentum but also positively highlighted Emily's role, enhancing her standing with Haruto and the executive leadership.

By combining these recommendations with an understanding of the unique challenges presented by The Amnesiac, professionals can develop a resilient approach that not only mitigates the effects of forgetfulness on project outcomes but also contributes to a more cohesive and effective working relationship.

Summing It Up

Navigating the challenges posed by The Amnesiac manager archetype requires a comprehensive and empathetic approach that combines proactive planning, strategic communication, and robust documentation. Understanding that forgetfulness at this level is often not intentional but rather a result of overwhelming responsibilities and cognitive overload is crucial for effective interaction. This chapter has provided insights into coping strategies designed to mitigate the impact of a forgetful manager on team dynamics and project success.

1. **Documentation and Strategic Communication:** First, creating a harmonious blend of enhanced documentation and strategic communication is vital. By using visual aids and repetitive reminders, you can help transition key concepts from your manager's short-term memory (RAM) to long-term memory (ROM). These visual tools act as mnemonic devices, ensuring that critical information is consistently reinforced and easily accessible. It's essential to establish a comprehensive system of documentation that records decisions, meetings, and key milestones, and to regularly integrate recaps and reminders into team communication.

2. **Engage With Empathy:** Secondly, engaging with empathetic persistence is key to fostering a supportive atmosphere conducive to positive outcomes. Acknowledging the pressures and workloads your manager faces allows you to approach interactions with understanding and patience. Steadily reinforcing key messages and revisiting agreed-upon decisions helps maintain a gentle yet firm approach to communication, ensuring that

crucial information remains at the forefront of discussions and decisions.

3. **Probe for Forgetfulness Ahead of Time:** Integrating feedback loops with adaptive project management tools presents a strategic approach to mitigating forgetfulness. Creating a safe and low-risk space for employees to probe and explore the degree to which The Amnesiac forgets about key projects, deliverables, and initiatives helps in preemptively addressing potential disruptions. Utilizing adaptive project management tools that allow for regular updates and visual tracking of project milestones ensures that key information remains accessible and top of mind for your manager.

By implementing these strategies, you can effectively manage The Amnesiac manager's forgetfulness, ensuring that vital information is retained and recalled when needed. This proactive approach not only preserves project momentum but also fosters a more supportive and collaborative work environment. Remember, combining empathy with structured communication and robust documentation is the key to transforming potential points of contention into opportunities for strengthening teamwork and leadership support.

CHAPTER 5

The Firefighter

Background

In the dimly lit conference room, Peter's gaze lingered on the wall, barely registering the ongoing discussion about quarterly forecasts. His mind wandered through the labyrinth of data he managed daily, contemplating the inefficiencies he'd grown accustomed to. The meeting, like many before, seemed an endless loop of projections and assurances.

Suddenly, his phone vibrated with an urgency that cut through the monotony. The message was terse: "System down. Customer accounts inaccessible. Emergency session now." Heart racing, Peter excused himself, his steps quickening as he headed toward the executive suite. The transition from the mundane to the critical was a strangely invigorating jolt to his system.

As he entered the emergency session, the atmosphere was palpable with tension. The executives turned to him, their expressions a mix of concern and expectation. Peter felt an unfamiliar surge of energy. For the first time in weeks, he felt crucial and alive. His team, including his vice presidents, rallied around him, drawing on his sudden vibrance. He listened, he directed, he decided. The crisis had kindled a fire within him, showcasing a version of himself that even he had forgotten existed.

Together, they navigated the chaos, piecing together a tactical response to the outage. Peter's directives were crisp, his decisions swift. The team was a well-oiled machine, fueled by his newfound dynamism. They were in awe of his transformation and his ability to thrive amidst the storm.

However, as the crisis abated and the system was restored, a palpable shift occurred in the days and weeks following the event. The adrenaline that had surged through Peter's veins dissipated, leaving a void in its wake. He retreated to his normal modus operandi of utilizing tactical, short-term, uncoordinated efforts and directives to address what clearly were long-term, strategic gaps in his workstreams and projects. His brief resurgence, born of the outage event, faded into a distant memory.

In the aftermath of the emergency, as the dust settled, Peter's team observed with growing concern his continued struggle to adapt to the demands of strategic leadership, despite his tactical victories during the outage. While the crisis had showcased his exceptional tactical acumen, his approach to the broader, long-term challenges facing their operations revealed a significant misalignment. Peter, still riding the wave of his recent success as a tactician, attempted to apply the same immediate, reactive problem-solving methods to complex issues that demanded a strategic, visionary approach. This misapplication highlighted a critical gap in his leadership repertoire. His team watched as he grappled unsuccessfully with this transition, unable to harness the strategic foresight and executive vision required to address systemic deficits and guide the team toward sustainable solutions. Peter's reliance on tactical responses in a landscape that necessitated deep, strategic planning underscored a pivotal learning curve he had yet to navigate, casting a shadow of uncertainty over his capacity to lead beyond the immediacy of crisis.

His team observed this transformation and reversion to his typical style with mixed feelings. They had seen what Peter was capable of and the leader he could be under pressure. Yet, as normalcy returned, so did his reluctance to embrace and grow in the realm of strategic thinking and executive leadership. It was disheartening to witness. They had been galvanized by his energy, inspired by his decisiveness, but now they grappled with the reality of a leader who shone brightest only in the heat of crisis.

The impact on the team was profound. The experience had bonded them, yet it also cast a shadow of longing for what could be. They had tasted the thrill of effective, energetic leadership, but the return to routine was a stark contrast. They understood the necessity of both tactical responses and strategic planning, but the disparity in Peter's engagement left them yearning for a balance that seemed out of reach.

The episode had been a revelation, a glimpse into the transformative power of leadership under fire. Yet, it also underscored the enduring challenge of sustaining that momentum, of bridging the gap between the immediacy of crisis management and the steady, forward-looking vision required for lasting success.

The Archetype Defined

At the heart of every organization lies a unique set of individuals whose true potential shines in the heat of crisis—these are The Firefighters. Renowned for their exceptional ability to remain calm under pressure and make swift decisions amidst chaos, firefighters become invaluable when unexpected challenges arise. Their almost instinctual knack for crisis management turns turmoil into order, embodying resilience and rapid problem-solving. However, this archetype presents a paradox in leadership: they excel during emergencies but often struggle with strategic foresight during calmer times.

The Firefighter is not just about responding to crises; they thrive on immediacy, prioritizing action over deliberation. Their tactical mindset is indispensable in dealing with disasters, yet this brilliance often overshadows their engagement with long-term planning. This creates a dichotomy between their performance in crises and periods of stability. Their ability to navigate emergencies with competence makes them a beacon of hope, but their focus on immediate responses can limit their effectiveness in addressing multifaceted strategic challenges. These individuals seem to come alive during a crisis, exhibiting proficiency in triaging, executing swiftly, and quelling the fire before it causes permanent damage. It's after the rescue and the fire is out that their struggle becomes apparent, as they often find it challenging to shift from emergency response to long-term strategic planning, leaving the team longing for direction and sustainable progress.

Working under a Firefighter leader can be exhilarating yet challenging. Teams draw inspiration from their decisiveness and energy during crises, but often struggle to engage, understand, and comply with their manager's seemingly random and ineffectual directives during quieter times. The Firefighter's emphasis on immediate issues can inadvertently create a void in long-term planning, making it difficult for teams to develop and adhere to a consistent strategy. This reactive approach can lead to missed opportunities, resource misallocation, and a sense of being constantly on edge, awaiting the next emergency.

Navigating the dynamic under a Firefighter leader involves a journey filled with both dedication and dissonance. Their focus on crisis management can frustrate those who push for strategic planning. This environment can stifle innovation and sap morale, as the team's energy is diverted from forward-thinking projects to addressing immediate fires. Ironically, the crises Firefighters excel at managing are often perpetuated by their reluctance to embrace preventative strategies. This creates a cycle of constant emergency response, limiting the organization's growth potential and eroding team motivation.

Studies highlight the negative impact of constant crisis management on long-term organizational stability and employee morale.[*] The challenge for teams working with Firefighter leaders is to balance the need for immediate action with the importance of long-term planning. By understanding the Firefighter's strengths and weaknesses, teams can better navigate this dynamic, fostering an environment where crises are managed effectively without sacrificing strategic vision.

Coping Strategies

While firefighting is going to be a part of every organization, it's important to attempt to infuse The Firefighter manager with the know how to transition from a posture of loving fires, to seeking to prevent them. Navigating the leadership style of a Firefighter manager requires a nuanced strategy of managing upward, guiding them toward the realization that prevention is more efficient than constant firefighting. Here are coping strategies designed to subtly shift their perspective and encourage a more strategic approach to leadership.

---

[*] Harvard Business Review, 2018, "Crisis Mode: Effects on Long-Term Organizational Stability," *Harvard Business Review*, https://hbr.org/2018/09/crisis-mode-effects-on-long-term-organizational-stability.

Emphasize the Value of Prevention Over Cure

Emphasizing the value of prevention over cure is crucial in shifting
The Firefighter manager's almost Pavlovian response from gaining energy
in crises to finding satisfaction in averting them. This paradigm shift
is arguably the most challenging aspect of dealing with this manager archetype, as it necessitates employing emotional intelligence to
subtly influence their perspective, rather than overwhelming them with
facts and data. By appealing to their sense of responsibility and the
deeper rewards of proactive leadership, you can begin to recalibrate
their instincts toward a more strategic, prevention-oriented mindset.
Employees must work to pivot a Firefighter's reward system, transitioning from the immediate gratification of extinguishing destructive fires
to the more nuanced satisfaction of preemptively preventing the harm
those fires could cause.

> **Initiate Strategic Debriefs (After Action Reports):** After every
> crisis, initiate a debrief session that not only celebrates the team's
> success in handling the situation but also focuses on analyzing
> the root causes of the fire. This fosters a culture of learning and
> continuous improvement.
> - Initiating strategic debriefs after crises bridges the gap between
>   reactive crisis management and proactive strategy, essen-
>   tial in environments led by Firefighter archetypes. This
>   method fosters a learning culture by analyzing crises to
>   uncover root causes and insights for improvement, enhanc-
>   ing team cohesion and promoting systemic problem-solving.
>   By focusing on both the cause of the fire and the areas
>   for growth, strategic debriefs encourage continuous improve-
>   ment, aligning with broader organizational objectives of
>   resilience and advancement.
> - As an employee under a Firefighter manager, you can champion
>   strategic debriefs by first acknowledging the team's success
>   in crisis resolution, then gently steering the conversation
>   toward constructive analysis. Begin by preparing a structured
>   debrief session outline that highlights key discussion points,

including what led to the crisis, the steps taken to resolve it, and potential preventive measures. Encourage open dialogue by asking insightful questions and inviting contributions from all team members. Document the findings and proposed strategies for prevention and offer to lead or participate in implementing these solutions. By taking the initiative in this way, you not only demonstrate leadership but also guide your manager and team toward a more strategic and preventive approach to challenges.

Showcase Prevention Successes: Collect and present case studies or instances where preventive measures averted potential crises in other teams or adjacent situations. Highlight these successes in team meetings or through internal communications to demonstrate the tangible benefits of strategic foresight that can be applied to your team's efforts. By referencing example cases, you can provide your manager with data that exemplifies how other teams met with success and growth by avoiding issues before they arise and develop into uncontrollable fires to be fought. If presented with empathy, you create a psychologically safe environment for your manager to explore a foreign concept with evidence of it working elsewhere.

Putting It Into Practice

Aisha watched as the last flickers of the emergency messages and emails waned, signaling the end of another crisis. She'd seen it again—Peter, usually so reserved, had transformed before her eyes, orchestrating the resolution of the platform outage with a fervor that was as impressive as it was intense. But as the adrenaline faded, so did the spark in Peter's eyes, replaced once more by a familiar, distant focus. Aisha had noticed a pattern: Peter thrived in chaos but seemed adrift in calm, and she couldn't help but feel that this cycle was a disservice to both her potential and the team's long-term success.

The next morning, Aisha approached Peter's office, pausing momentarily before knocking.

Aisha: "Peter, got a minute?" she asked, stepping inside.

Peter: "Sure, Aisha. What's on your mind?"

Aisha: "It's about the outage yesterday. You were incredible, Peter. You really come alive in those moments. But I've been thinking … what if we could prevent these fires altogether?"

Peter's expression shifted, a mix of defensiveness and curiosity.

Peter: "Prevent? Aisha, we handle what comes at us. That's the job. We have to be ready to react and dive into the thick of it," he confessed, almost reluctantly.

Aisha: "I know, I know. But imagine if we could channel a small portion of that energy into prevention. Not only handling crises but stopping them before they start. It's what Haruto and the executives really expect from us—to not just be firefighters but guardians."

Peter was silent, the idea conflicting with the adrenaline rush he'd come to rely on.

Aisha: "Here's a thought. What if we started doing postmortems after every major incident? Really dig into the why and how, then report our findings to the executives, focusing on how we plan to prevent similar issues. It's about changing our mindset, Peter. From reacting to preventing."

Peter pondered as the idea of prevention began to dismantle his resistance.

Peter: "It seems like a waste of time to me. What good is it to spend time analyzing the fires we've already put out? We need to spend time getting ready for the next one."

Aisha: "I can see your point that focusing on the past might not yield obvious value, but here's the critical point that I'm trying to get you to see. I'm totally on board with being prepared in advance to help fight fires. But just like at your home, you take measures to prevent fires from happening. You have fire extinguishers, smoke alarms, and an evacuation plan, but you make sure to practice fire safety in everything you do so a fire doesn't happen. We should do the same here. And when a fire does happen, you absolutely need to know what caused it so that it doesn't happen again, right?"

Peter paused, leaning back in his chair, attempting to find a vector of conversation that would squelch what felt like a proposal from Aisha to be less ready for emergencies.

Peter: "Aisha, I get where you're coming from. But our team is built for action, for response. Diving into analytics and prevention … it feels like we're stepping back from the front lines. Isn't our strength in dealing with crises as they come?"

Aisha sensed his hesitance and attachment to the identity of a crisis manager. She leaned in slightly, her voice softening, tapping into a deep well of empathy and emotional intelligence.

Aisha: "Peter, think about the team for a moment. Yes, we're built for action, and we've proven ourselves time and again. But consider the toll it takes—on you, on everyone. The constant state of high alert, the adrenaline rushes, and then the crashes. We're always reacting, but rarely do we ask, 'How can we stop this from happening again?'"

Peter met her gaze, the defense slowly crumbling as the truth of her words sunk in.

Aisha: "You're an incredible leader in a crisis, Peter. No one can take that from you. But imagine leading a team that's equally incredible at preventing crises. The energy you feel when we're in the thick of it? We can channel that into building something proactive, something sustainable. This isn't about stepping back; it's about stepping up. Being guardians, not just firefighters."

Peter's resistance wavered, Aisha's words painting a picture of a future he hadn't allowed himself to consider—one where his role evolved beyond the cycle of crisis response.

Aisha "Haruto sees the potential in us to be more, Peter. He's asking for this shift because he believes in our ability to adapt, to grow. And I believe in you. You've led us through fires, now let's lead in preventing them. Let's use those postmortems not as a look back in regret but as a strategic tool for a safer, more efficient future."

Peter sat in silence, wrestling with a mix of emotions. Finally, he
nodded, a slow, deliberate movement that marked the beginning
of a new chapter.

Peter "Alright, Aisha. Let's draft an agenda for a postmortem of the
last issue we addressed. Let's demonstrate to Haruto that we're
not just about fighting fires—we're about safeguarding our team,
our platform, from the flames altogether."

Aisha "I'm confident that this is the right choice, Peter. This … this
is going to be good for us. For everyone."

Note how in this interaction, Aisha is planting the seeds of cultural
change by attempting to propose to Peter that converting from a
methodology of reaction (and all the immediate rewards that might
seem to provide) to prevention is a much more rewarding strategy.
Additionally, using empathy and understanding of Peter's entrenched
disposition on the topic, he's proposing a low-risk way to analyze the
root causes of a failure in the hopes that it might lead to insights on how
to take actions proactively to avoid them in the future. This new way of
thinking can position Peter and his team in the mind of key executives
as a forward leaning, mature team to be counted on to safeguard the
organization's platforms and capabilities, rather than just run around
and put out fires, leaving a damaged landscape of metaphorical burned
scaffolding behind them. Also note how Aisha utilizes the postmortem
strategy of not just breathing a sigh of relief after a fire is extinguished,
but she is trying to get Peter to see that learning from the failure,
defining the root cause, and then reporting out on preventative measures
that will be taken in the future is what the organization and executive
leadership really needs.

Formalize a Culture of Proactive Problem-Solving With Ceremonies

To guide a Firefighter manager toward the prevention paradigm,
employees can use specific, actionable practices that not only encourage
this shift but also support the manager in developing the necessary
strategic muscles. This transition is pivotal, requiring the manager to

learn and embrace behavior changes that counter their instinctual draw toward crisis management.

Establishing ceremonies like proactive prevention forums, anchored by a robust tracking system, serves as a vivid showcase of how the team has successfully averted disaster, underscoring the tangible benefits of preemptive action. These ceremonies act as a forcing function, compelling the Firefighter manager to confront their instinctual draw toward crisis management and instead, gradually pivot toward a strategic focus on prevention. With the inclusion of executive leadership in these sessions, the manager is not only encouraged to attend and engage but is also provided with a platform to align their actions with broader organizational goals, reinforcing the shift toward a preventive mindset.

Encourage Proactive Reporting: Develop a system for reporting potential issues before they escalate into fires. Use these reports as a basis for discussion in one-on-ones with The Firefighter manager, framing them as opportunities for strategic improvement. Employees can take the initiative by setting up a structured, user-friendly system for identifying and reporting potential issues early. This could involve creating simple yet comprehensive reporting templates or utilizing digital platforms that allow for real-time issue tracking. The key is to make this process as accessible and straightforward as possible, encouraging widespread adoption within the team.

- Once the system is in place, employees should actively use the collected data to engage The Firefighter manager in one-on-one discussions. Instead of presenting these reports as mere problems that need solutions, frame them as opportunities for strategic improvement. For example, an employee might say, "I've noticed a recurring issue with X, which could lead to bigger problems down the line. I believe we have an opportunity here to address it proactively. Here are some potential strategies we could consider.…"

Highlight Long-Term Impact: Use data and analytics to show how preventive strategies can lead to better outcomes, such as improved team morale, increased productivity, and cost savings. This evidentiary approach can help in persuading a Firefighter leader of the value of strategic thinking.

To reinforce the value of a preventive approach, employees can gather data and analytics that illustrate the tangible benefits of addressing issues proactively. This might involve conducting a case study on a recent intervention that prevented a potential crisis, showcasing metrics such as time saved, cost reductions, or productivity improvements.

All of these elements can be components of the monthly or quarterly prevention report to the organization and key business owners and executives. In this way, the Prevention Forum outlined before can be the place where these data-driven conclusions can be presented and generate support for even more strategic, meaningful prevention activities.

Putting It Into Practice

Aisha waited until Peter joined the video meeting. He looked up from his cluttered desk, still surrounded by remnants of their latest crisis management success.

Peter: "Hey Aisha. What's on your mind?"

Aisha took a deep breath, readying her pitch.

Aisha: "I've been thinking about our conversation on moving toward a prevention-focused approach. I'm really happy that we've got your support to go down this road. I know we've agreed tentatively to prepare postmortem root causes analyses for each issue. I see the value in tactical responses, but I'm also enthused about sharpening our pivot toward being more strategic. We've got to take some real first steps above and beyond just saying we'll report on prevention. We need to start practicing it."

Peter: "I remember this and have been struggling a bit. How do you propose we track our success, if not by the fires we put out?"

Aisha smiled, glad to see him considering the proposal.

Aisha: "What about a Prevention Success Forum. We track and celebrate our days without incident and present our prevention strategies in our monthly and quarterly reviews. We show the executives that we're not just solving problems, but we're ahead of them."

Peter leaned back, the gears turning. The concept was foreign, yet undeniably appealing.

Peter: "Prevention as our metric of success. ... It's a shift," he admitted.

Aisha nodded, encouraged by his openness. She'd gotten him to a place where he was willing to listen to alternative viewpoints.

Aisha: "Exactly. We get to show how we're safeguarding our platform, not just rescuing it. The postmortems are the first baby step. Those postmortems need to translate into proactive steps that we take in our daily jobs. It's a more sustainable approach, Peter. For us and for the organization. A Prevention Success Forum, attended by Haruto and the leadership team will be just the right disaster prevention council and audience for us to report on our efforts."

Peter: "I'm still concerned though Aisha. We are built to deal with these issues. If we focus on pivoting, I'm afraid that we'll dull ourselves in a crisis and we won't be able to respond effectively."

Aisha: "That's completely understandable. It would stand to reason that if we try to change ourselves, we could be less effective at the very thing that we're good at, which is fighting fires. However, think about after you've moved on from this team after leading it successfully. How do you want to leave it? Do you want to say I've put out x number of fires over the last five years, or would you rather have leadership say that not only did Peter put out the fires, but he and his team prevented so many more, safeguarding the organization from harm?"

Peter met her gaze, a newfound resolve beginning to take shape.

Peter: "Alright, Aisha. Let's draft up a plan for this Prevention Success Forum. It's going to be a challenge, changing our stripes from firefighters to guardians. I just don't want us to expend too much energy that would sap our focus on being ready...."

Aisha: "I think this is the right move Peter. Why don't I set up a simple prevention tracking spreadsheet, linking the postmortem conclusions to key actions we can take to prevent the same type of fire from happening again? We'll quickly outgrow a spreadsheet if this is successful, but it's a low risk and low effort way of getting started."

Peter: "That sounds OK to me. Let me know when you have the first draft, and I can get busy scheduling a review with Haruto."

Notice how Aisha is utilizing empathy to put herself in Peter's position by restating his trepidation and reservations with each response. Also, note how Aisha expertly addresses a common flaw in this specific manager archetype's thinking. The logical flaw is that if the team does anything else proactively to prevent the fires from arising, the effort required to support prevention takes effort away from the hypervigilance required to spring into action when a fire does break out. This thinking perpetually keeps the team in firefighting, react-only mode and often squashes any effort to prevent fires for fear of being less responsive and less effective in a fire. Notice how Aisha addresses this flaw by assuring that this prevention effort, starting with a simple spreadsheet, requiring minimum effort will yield remarkable results that aligns with a mature executive leader's desire to eliminate as many fires as possible. She assures Peter that the team can do two things at the same time, eventually leading to a reduction in fires altogether.

Drive the Prevention Mindset

Driving a prevention mindset in Firefighter managers is most effective when they are momentarily distanced from their day-to-day operational duties, providing a unique vantage point to witness, learn, and cultivate prevention-based thinking skills. This process essentially involves creating a safe space where their firefighting instincts can be subtly redirected toward proactive measures, thereby not just encouraging but actively demonstrating the value of strategic foresight. As an employee, leveraging such opportunities to manage upward allows you to guide your manager's participation, fostering a collaborative environment where preventive thinking becomes a shared goal and practice.

>**Strategic Brainstorming Sessions:** Organize regular meetings focused on strategic planning and invite your manager to participate. Use these sessions to brainstorm preventive measures for known issues and to develop long-term strategies for growth and improvement. This can include reviewing the highest priority items from the tracking system identified previously as a means to immerse the team in creative and expansive methods of thinking to develop more holistic, systems-oriented solutions to preventing issues. By making room to ideate in this manner, effectively taking your team and your recovering Firefighter manager out of their day-to-day activities, they can more freely spend cycles on proactive, prevention-based strategies. Document these ideas and decompose them into "features" that can be assigned to workstreams and program managed for implementation.

Note that this may be slow going at first. Be sure to monitor and draw in your Firefighting manager as strategic thinking typically does not offer the same reward and excitement as putting out fires. If not managed adequately, they may disengage from the planning sessions and only be there physically, instead of mentally. Take particular care to engage them, involving them in structured activities, have them lead discussions and summarize outcomes. The more engaged they are, the more they won't shut down on the session and eventually call it ineffective.

>**Create a Feedback Loop:** Establish a mechanism for ongoing feedback on strategic initiatives, making it a two-way street where the manager's insights and experiences in crisis management are valued and integrated into broader strategic plans. Pressure test their progress in transitioning away from firefighting thinking to prevention thinking. Apply empathetic influence if you sense

during these feedback loops that they are not engaged and focused in the right manner.

Putting It Into Practice

Aisha and Peter settled into the quiet conference room, the morning sunlight casting a warm glow over the table. Aisha had prepared meticulously for this half-day strategy session, understanding the potential it held for shaping Peter's approach to leadership. Looking around the room at the combined team, many of whom he'd already spoken to about the real goal of the strategy session, she looked forward to leveraging their support in changing Peter's mindset away from firefighting to strategic prevention.

> **Aisha:** "Thanks everyone for being here today. I know it's not easy to carve out this time during our busy day, but this is critical. I'm especially excited that Peter has committed to joining us today and actively participating in this new way of strategizing how our team operates. I know stepping away from the day-to-day isn't easy, but I believe this time is crucial for us. Let's make it a laptops-closed exercise and really focus on the here and now, free from distractions."

Peter, visibly uneasy without his usual digital armor, nodded reluctantly, closing his laptop with a soft click.

> **Aisha:** "I'd like us to start by envisioning our team a year from now. Imagine we've successfully minimized our crisis interventions by half. What steps did we take to get there? How did we pull it off?"

Peter fidgeted, his mind instinctively racing to the adrenaline-fueled moments of crisis management that defined so much of his leadership style. While a few of Aisha's team volunteered constructive and compelling answers, she noticed how Peter appeared to be staring into space at the prospect of thinking that far ahead. Aisha directly asked him for his thoughts. Peter looked around the room, as if awakening from his mental disconnection and responded.

Peter: "Well, I suppose … we'd have to really understand what triggers these crises so we can fight them more efficiently."

Aisha: "That's a good start, recognizing triggers. Let's dig deeper. Preventing fires isn't just about a better response; it's about removing the fuel before the fire starts. For example, if we notice a pattern in system overloads leading to outages, how could we address the root cause?"

Peter paused, considering Aisha's analogy, his gears slowly shifting.

Peter: "Okay, so if we strengthened our monitoring systems by introducing predictive analytics, we could anticipate and mitigate those overloads before they become critical."

Aisha: "Exactly! That's preventive thinking. It's about shifting from reaction to action. Now, how could we apply that mindset to our team's workflow?"

As the session progressed, Aisha gently guided Peter through various scenarios, each designed to challenge his firefighting instincts and encourage a proactive stance. With every suggestion Peter made, Aisha offered encouragement and refinement, modeling the strategic foresight she hoped to instill.

Peter, gradually warming to the exercise, began to see the potential in this new approach. The initial resistance gave way to a cautious enthusiasm as he started connecting the dots, envisioning a team less burdened by crises and more focused on innovation and stability.

Peter: "You know, Aisha, I'm starting to see how this could work. It's a bit like chess, isn't it? Anticipating moves, planning several steps ahead."

Aisha smiled, pleased to see the spark of understanding in Peter's eyes.

Aisha: "Exactly like chess. And the beauty of it is, the more we practice thinking this way, the better we become at it. It's about building a new kind of muscle, one that flexes before a crisis even hints at emerging."

By the end of the session, Peter had not only engaged with the concept of preventive strategies but had also begun to embrace it. Thanks to Aisha's persistence and the safe space he'd created for exploration and learning, Peter took the first crucial steps toward evolving his leadership style from reactive firefighting to strategic prevention.

By implementing these coping mechanisms, you can help shift a Firefighter manager's perspective toward recognizing the importance of strategic foresight and preventive measures. The goal is to transform the adrenaline-driven satisfaction of crisis resolution into a deeper fulfillment derived from cultivating stability, resilience, and strategic growth within the organization.

Summing It Up

The Firefighter manager archetype, characterized by a penchant for diving headlong into crises and emerging victorious, faces a pivotal shift in perspective. The challenge lies not in extinguishing fires with valor but in nurturing a landscape where fires seldom ignite. This evolution requires a fundamental change in how success is measured and celebrated within teams led by Firefighter managers.

1. **Track Days Without Incident:** Adopting a "days without incident" scorecard marks a transformative step in this journey. It represents a tangible metric that shifts focus from reactive heroism to proactive stability. This scorecard becomes a badge of honor, celebrating not the rapid quenching of fires but the foresight and strategic planning that prevented those fires from starting. It's a transition from a hero complex, addicted to the rush of crisis resolution, to a guardian ethos that takes pride in the tranquility of order and safety.

2. **Proactive Problem-Solving Ceremonies:** Proactive problem-solving will be a cultural shift for The Firefighter. One of the best

ways to shift culture can be to implement key ceremonies that are small, recurring and reinforcing sets of behavior that accrue to a shift in mindset, especially for The Firefighter manager. Each time the manager participates or hears about a ceremony, it cements the fact that the team is changing for the better.

3. **An Ounce of Prevention:** Prevention being better than a cure is a crucial extension of the ceremony-based proactive shifts that are essential to help The Firefighter manager grow. While initially resistant to this type of thinking, largely because they believe their strength and value is managing crises, helping them transition to speaking about how they prevented disasters as an alternative badge of honor will help them grow professionally.

For the Firefighter manager, these coping strategies will engender a deep, introspective relinquishment of the adrenaline-fueled victories in favor of a quieter, more sustained triumph—preventive victory. It means redefining leadership success to value the anticipation of challenges and the implementation of strategies that mitigate risk and enhance resilience. This new measure of success encourages a culture of vigilance and continuous improvement, where each day without incident is a testament to effective leadership and strategic foresight.

This approach fosters a more stable, predictable work environment conducive to innovation, efficiency, and employee satisfaction. It minimizes burnout and turnover by eliminating the constant stress of emergency situations, thereby enhancing team cohesion and organizational loyalty.

In sum, the transformation of the Firefighter manager into a strategic guardian is both a personal and organizational journey toward sustainability and growth. It's about building a legacy of stability, foresight, and strategic resilience—celebrating victories not in the fires extinguished but in the fires that never needed to be fought. This philosophical pivot not only enriches the manager's leadership repertoire but also fortifies the team and the organization against the unpredictable flames of tomorrow's challenges.

CHAPTER 6

The Order Taker

Background

In the polished corridors of the organization's corporate headquarters executive office suite, anticipation hung thick in the air, not unlike a dense fog that blankets the city at dawn. Today was the day of the much-anticipated product review session led by Alison, the organization's chief data officer, whose reputation for sharp insights and uncompromising standards preceded her. Her domain, the intersection of product management and business needs relating to all things data, was both a battleground and a fertile ground for innovation.

As they entered the lush executive conference room, Keisha could sense Hannah's tension. She long had observed her relationship with Alison as one in which Hannah exhibited an extraordinary amount of deference to Alison's demands, wishes, and directives. Keisha knew that while Alison was the chief data officer, she required a true partner to pressure test her directives, ideas, and desires and to advise and guide their implementation, rather than just saying "yes" because of her seniority within the organization. This morning, Hannah found herself challenged yet again. As the managing vice president and head of engineering, she was Alison's counterpart in transforming visionary ideas into tangible assets that propelled the organization forward. It was her team that did the work to make Alison's directives real. However, the symbiosis between them, while ideal on paper, was riddled with complexities, much like the software architectures and systems that Hannah's team wrestled to support daily.

As a seasoned vice president with a background in the technology industry, Keisha watched the dynamics of their relationship play out yet again with a sense of foreboding. As Alison went through some of the challenges the organization was facing based on engineering issues with the platform owned by Hannah's team, she realized that demanding more new features, instead of allotting time to fix existing issues would further decrease the platform's stability. Her experience lent her a perspective that was both a gift and a curse. While she saw the potential in Hannah and Alison's partnership, she also saw the pitfalls. Deferring to demands, instead of providing guidance, grounding, and opportunity cost was a detriment to the team and the organization's success. Today, she watched as Alison rolled on, unconstrained and unchallenged in her demands.

As Alison detailed the next wave of product features, her words were a clarion call to innovation. Yet, Hannah's responses, while supportive, echoed with the weight of unspoken challenges. Keisha's concerns were palpable; she knew that within each "yes" from Hannah was a silent acknowledgment of the significant efforts their entire team would have to muster. Not just to build anew, but to maintain, secure, and innovate within the bounds of an ever-tightening resource pool of personnel.

The technical debt, a term as innocuous as it was misleading, loomed large over Hannah's team. It was the shadow cast by past innovations, a toll that demanded to be paid in time, effort, and the currency of opportunity cost. Security holes, compliance with cybersecurity mandates—these were not just line items on a project plan. They were the hard realities that Keisha wished Hannah would share with Alison, not to push back, but to partner in the truest sense. To be fair, Keisha realized that without this knowledge and the implications of the growing amount of technical debt (a term used to describe how much the team would have to fix after they released new capabilities), Alison would just continue to make demands for new capabilities. She would proceed with her envisioned future state, blissfully ignorant of the detrimental impact the new orders she was issuing would have on the existing platform despite Hannah just blindly agreeing to them.

As the meeting unfolded, Hannah's instinct to accommodate and be differential, perhaps due to Alison's organizational seniority, led her to continue to take the path of least resistance. In the face of Alison's driven focus, Keisha was disheartened. She saw in Hannah not the lack of understanding but perhaps a reluctance to confront, educate, and lead, not just her team but also Alison, toward a more sustainable path.

The meeting adjourned with plans made and actions set. Yet, for Keisha, the resolution was anything but satisfactory. She saw the toll it would take, not just on the team but on Hannah herself. Her role as an order taker, as she saw it, diminished the true potential of what true collaboration and partnership could achieve. It was a pattern all too familiar, where immediate demands overshadowed long-term viability, and partnership gave way to unilateral direction.

The Archetype Defined

In the labyrinthine corridors of the workplace, where ambition, vision, and directions intertwine with the pragmatics of execution, resides a figure emblematic of acquiescence—The Order Taker. This archetype is not so much defined by their own vision as they are sculpted by the demands and directives that flow downward from the echelons above. Unlike the trailblazers or the strategists who forge partnerships and navigate the relationships between requirements, resources, and cost with the compass of their conviction and strategy, The Order Taker is like a vessel at sea that is rudderless, going where the waves take it.

The Order Taker prioritizes harmony over conflict, often at the cost of their own professional voice. They navigate through storms by adjusting the sails rather than questioning the course, embodying the mantra of "ask how, not why." Operating under the direct sway of their superiors, they are often seen less as the captains of their domain and more as lieutenants, executing orders with precision but seldom questioning their strategic merit.

The tragedy is that even if they are capable, willing, and disciplined enough to develop their own strategic vision, which could balance the needs of the organization, they often quickly abandon these principles when another vertical mandate is issued. Seemingly abandoning all strategic focus, they accept the new orders without question and become immersed in the tactics of execution, regardless of what storms may be on the horizon. The Order Taker becomes laser focused intensely on the immediate future, often sacrificing the broader vistas of opportunity and innovation. Their world is one of tasks, which lead to abandoned visions, or one of checkboxes, instead of frontiers. It may make employees and team members feel that in the face of executive demands, The Order Taker archetype not only immediately accepts the orders but also asks "do you want fries with that?"

Almost immediately after abandoning strategic vision to support executive deference and harmony, The Order Taker's landscape becomes dotted with the immediate and the urgent, often leading to a jarring reassignment of resources that prioritizes present demands over sustained, stable, and often committed work. A study by Deloitte revealed that teams lose approximately 25 percent of their productivity when switching between projects.[*] Managers who overload their teams with constant switches risk compromising productivity, quality, and team cohesion. This accumulates each time it happens, building up "organizational bad cholesterol," that will result in negative impacts to the team, the personnel and the organization.

As this organizational cholesterol accumulates, it has an impact on team morale and dynamics while building frustration, fragmenting focus, and leaving team members wondering when the next catastrophic interruption will occur. It may lead employees to feel dissatisfied that their work never gets completed because they are snatched away to hop onto the latest new tactical mandate following an executive meeting. What The Order Taker seeks to build is a calm sea of compliance and harmony with executive mandates, despite the tumultuous nature of reality roiling beneath the veneer. Beneath the team's surface of compliance and execution lies a tumultuous sea of missed opportunities and unvoiced concerns. The Order Taker, in their pursuit of immediate execution, often forgoes the chance to advocate for their team's innovative potential, to negotiate the balance between what is demanded, what is possible, and what is advisable. They risk becoming a simple cog in a machine that is about to burn out and collapse under its own weight, rather than the hand that steers it.

---

[*] Deloitte Consulting LLP. n.d. "Fixing the Overload Problem at Work." Deloitte Insights. Accessed May 21, 2024.

Coping Strategies

The journey from order-taking to partnership is fraught with challenges but like with many other archetypes, managers can grow beyond it. It begins with the cultivation of a strategic voice, one that seeks not only to understand the directives but also to contextualize them within the broader narrative of the team's capacity and vision. It involves the courage to question, negotiate, and propose alternatives that marry the immediate with the important, while realizing that this courage isn't disharmonious, but in fact is ground for constructing lasting partnerships with executive leadership.

The Order Taker has the potential to evolve, to blend their inherent skills of execution and diplomacy with a newfound strategic assertiveness. In doing so, they can transform from the echo of their superiors' directives into a pivotal force that shapes the trajectory of their team and, ultimately, the organization.

Highlight the Impact of Excessive Compliance (Order-Taking)

At the core of coping with an Order Taker manager is getting them to realize the impact of their behavior on their own team as it relates to team outputs, results, performance, and morale as well as the team's ability to achieve demonstrable objectives. All of this is in danger when a spate of new "orders" come in from executive leadership who often doesn't understand the implications of their new demands. To get The Order Taker manager to see this, however, requires gentle empathy and humility. These are essential tools to convince the manager to listen. If not done correctly, The Order Taker manager may see any suggestions as an admonishment of their skills and capabilities and reject the change.

> **Share Stories:** The key is to get this manager archetype into a place where they are willing to listen. An effective way to do this is by sharing stories about the impact of a recent order-taking activity. Without root causing the issue, highlight a challenge or series of challenges experienced by the team under the manager as a

result of their behavior, without ascribing the difficulty directly to them yet. Collect anecdotal evidence from the team where sudden shifts in focus have disrupted work or led to incomplete tasks. Sharing specific examples can help personalize the issue and highlight the real-world consequences of nonstrategic compliance. By personalizing the issue, especially attaching the emotional toll it's taken on those involved, you can help encourage The Order Taker to empathize with their team's difficulties.

Back It Up With Data: Once The Order Taker has a full appreciation for the team's challenges as a result of their order-taking behavior, in the same session, or a separate one, compile a data set that shows the impact of the stories. For each story, identify how many times a similar event has occurred within the team, and the impact or cost of that event in terms of dollars, hours, and morale.

For example, highlighting an incident where a new requirement comes in after a leadership meeting and disrupts a team member working on a key project, feature, or capability means that there is an opportunity cost in terms of dollars. Highlight what the cost of the organization not receiving the feature is, in favor of refocusing and context switching the engineer to the new task, leaving the other one "floating in the ether."

Create detailed reports or presentations that show the timeline and resource allocation of past and current projects. Highlight instances where excessive compliance has led to neglect of strategic initiatives or left critical work unfinished. Use visual aids such as Gantt charts or resource allocation grids to make this information clear and impactful. Using the Gantt chart can be effective especially if you chart the infusion of new requirements or projects as milestones along the timeline. You'll have a visual that easily demonstrates the impact of the new requirements (fresh from an order-taking leadership meeting) and how they impact critical initiatives that the team is responsible for.

Putting It Into Practice

Keisha: "Hannah, thank you for meeting with me today. I want to share some observations and feedback from our team that might help us improve our project outcomes and team satisfaction."

Hannah: "Of course, Keisha. I'm always open to hearing about ways we can improve, but I'm sensing some bad news coming.… "

Keisha: "Actually I think it's good news! I've identified an issue, and I think I have my arms around it. I've been collecting some feedback and stories from the team about the deluge of repeated shifts in our project focus. For example, there was an instance where an engineer was pulled from developing a critical security feature to address an urgent request from last week's leadership meeting. The feature was near completion, and now it's on hold."

Hannah: "I remember that. Alison told us in our leadership monthly update that her request was urgent. We didn't really have any other choice but to address it immediately based on the directives we received. The team has to be able to be responsive when we get leadership mandates."

Keisha: "Absolutely. Sometimes we have to put things on hold and prioritize and I get that, but when it becomes excessive, it can have a negative impact on the team. In this latest instance, while the response was aligned with Alison's immediate demand, the team felt the impact deeply. The security feature was crucial not just for our product but for customer trust. Pausing it has delayed our timeline and, according to my calculations, could potentially cost us in terms of both customer satisfaction and direct financial implications if a breach occurs."

Hannah: "That's a significant concern. How is this the first time I'm hearing about this? You said this is happening a lot. Do we know how often this has occurred?"

Keisha: "That's actually part of what I wanted to show you today."

Keisha presents a Gantt chart of project executions with an overlay of delays versus their original execution time frames. Against the backdrop of the various bars, she points out the meetings with Alison, correlating them to project delays.

Keisha: "Here's a visual representation of our projects over the last quarter. Each red line here indicates where we've had to shift focus. You can see the overlap and how each shift has left projects like the security feature incomplete. Also, note that these delays coincide directly with meetings where requirements from Alison are held."

Hannah: "Are you saying that each time we get requirements from Alison, the projects that we're working on are delayed? I hadn't realized the cumulative effect of these changes."

Keisha: "And that's understandable given the pace at which we operate. Each of these instances where we pivot might seem necessary in the moment, but they add up, impacting not just our deliverables but our team's morale. They've expressed feeling unsettled, unable to complete tasks to the best of their ability, which in turn affects their satisfaction and performance."

Hannah: "I get it, but I just don't see any other way of doing things. Alison sets the tempo and gives us the directions. Our team has to deliver. We can't just tell her we won't work on what she wants because we're busy on other things."

Keisha pauses, giving the appearance of listening, even though she has anticipated this response from Hannah. This puts her into a place where they're both working through the problem, rather than Keisha preaching a preconceived solution to her.

Keisha: "What if we could balance understanding Alison and listening to her needs, but also protect our existing work? We could focus on mitigating the impact to the team, but I first think we need more information. While this Gannt view is helpful, it doesn't capture the deep impact to the team's morale. I've shared with you just one story today about the impact, but there have got to be others. Maybe I'll collect some more evidence and then work on finding the right way to balance new requirements from Alison with our existing work that is crucial to the organization."

Hannah: "That sounds fine Keisha, but we have to keep in mind that we can't tell Alison 'no, we're not going to do something.' We have to find a way to complete our tasks but be ready for new work."

Keisha: "Understood Hannah. Let me come back to you with some data that outlines the impact of this situation and a recommendation on how we can proceed."

Note how in this conversation, Keisha exposes Hannah to the challenges the team is feeling by providing a single example of the latest disruptive injection of requirements from Alison (facilitated by Hannah, but she never accuses her directly). Also note how she provides a data-driven view of how these requirements are visibly delaying projects, including putting the entire organization at risk. Keisha doesn't beat Hannah over the head with an accusation that her order-taking is the source of the issue, but she paints a backdrop so that they both become aware that there is an issue that clearly needs to be solved. She also takes note that Hannah is committed to never saying "no" to Alison, which indicates that she has a challenge ahead of her in educating her on how to establish a true partnership. Again, also note how Keisha takes it upon herself to do the research and synthesize the data for their next interaction.

Sharp observers will see how Hannah uttered the dreaded question "How is this the first time I'm hearing about this," calling back to The Surprised manager archetype as well. Note how Keisha doesn't address that here and continues to drive toward working with Hannah.

Connect Unfinished Commitments to Team Performance and Organizational Impact

Once the manager understands the emotional and intangible team impact as well as how that turns into quantifiable commitment delays based on the infusion of newly accepted and immediately prioritized requirements from leadership, capitalize on their willingness to hear more. The goal will be to paint a picture that illustrates that unless something changes, this disruptive behavior will likely have additional detrimental team, performance, and result impacts that extend to harming the organization. You need to get The Order Taker manager to see that if the team swiftly abandons their commitments to valuable organizational work in favor of the latest demands that have not been vetted and prioritized, this will hurt not just the team, but the organization as a whole.

> **Quantify the Impact:** In the previous coping strategy, we focused on gathering stories and anecdotes to illustrate the emotional impact of the order-taking behavior on the team. We edged closer to providing data in terms of cost associated with those stories. Now, in this coping strategy, we need to educate The Order Taker on the magnitude of their behavior. Provide concrete data on how unfinished tasks have directly affected team performance metrics and organizational goals. For example, show how all incomplete or abandoned projects due to diverted resources pose risks to the company. Make sure to find a way to articulate it in terms of dollars and effort (hours).

> **Future Forecasting:** The Order Taker must also understand that there are going to be new executive meetings where additional requirements will flow down from leadership. Help The Order Taker understand that each time this occurs, if the demands are agreed to wholesale, there will be anticipated significant team and organizational impact. For example, prepare a visual to predict the outcomes if strategic projects continue to be sidelined, including potential losses in efficiency, revenue, or market position.

Refrain from painting a doom and gloom-based scenario, but index on the realities of the situation. At the same time, remain positive and upbeat, indicating that there is a better way to handle demands from leadership with finite team resources, while at the same time, not balking at those demands based on existing workloads. This sets the stage for helping The Order Taker manager into understanding how to forge and behave in partnerships.

Putting It Into Practice

Keisha: "Hannah, I appreciate you taking the time for this discussion. As promised, I've been analyzing our team's workflow and I've noticed a pattern that's becoming increasingly problematic, especially as it relates to team morale."

Hannah emits a pent-up sigh, obviously not looking forward to this discussion nor Keisha's findings, but because Keisha has already communicated the impact of the phenomenon on the team, she knows that she needs to listen.

Hannah: "Okay, let's have it."

Keisha: "It's about the cycle of accepting new projects and tasks without fully assessing their impact on our current commitments. When we shift our focus too quickly, it not only delays our ongoing strategic projects but also increases our risk, like with the incomplete security updates we've sidelined."

Hannah: "I see your point, Keisha, but as I told you last time, we need to meet the leadership's demands. They expect quick action on new requirements. Saying 'no' is not an option."

Keisha: "Absolutely, meeting leadership demands is crucial. However, the immediate prioritization of these tasks is costing us in ways that aren't always apparent on the surface. And I'm sure Alison doesn't know the impact of some of these sacrifices. For instance, by diverting our finite resources to these new demands, we've delayed critical updates. This could pose significant security risks, potentially costing us not just time but substantial financial resources in the event of a breach."

Hannah: "Yes, but these seem like reasons why we won't comply though...."

Keisha: "I thought you might say that, so I tried to quantify exactly how not finishing this particular commitment would cost the organization. Consider the security patch updates we postponed last month. I've done a rough calculation, and the delay increases our exposure to potential breaches, which could cost us upward of $200,000 in containment alone, not to mention the loss of customer trust and potential revenue."

Hannah: "That's concerning, but that's the nature of our jobs. We take direction from leadership. What else can we do?"

Keisha: "If I'm in Alison's position, she might not understand the implication of us simply saying 'yes' and what that actually means as it relates to existing work. If we keep saying 'yes' and pushing existing work, she'll eventually begin to ask why things are taking so long to complete. I suggest we listen and understand her requirements, but at the same time, help her understand when we can get to it. That way we're not saying 'no,' we're just forecasting when she'll see them while equipping her with an understanding of why it's not right now."

Hannah: "She's already doing that. I have an email from her asking when the security update will be completed, even though she asked us to do five new things during our last leadership connection meeting."

Keisha: "You've just identified the challenge perfectly. There is a way out. We have to educate her on the impact of her requests against existing work. It's not saying no, but it's focusing on scheduling the work. But it requires us to be courageous enough not to just accept these demands. We need to be her partner and advise her of the implications of a limited pool of resources like our team."

Hannah: "Instead of 'no,' its 'not right now'?"

Keisha: "Exactly. I think a structured approach to managing incoming tasks would benefit us. Each time a new request comes in, we could add it to a managed backlog. Then, we could assess its priority against our current projects in a bi-weekly review meeting. This way, we can make informed decisions that balance new demands with ongoing commitments. And during our leadership connection meetings, we can advise Alison, so she has the full picture of what her asks are against committed work. If she disagrees with our priorities, she can then advise us to reprioritize, but she does so with the full knowledge of what the costs and impacts of that choice are."

Hannah: "It gives us a chance to evaluate the impact of new tasks more holistically, while educating Alison on what it will take to do what she's asking."

Keisha: "You got it. And it's not just about managing risks; it's also about preserving our team's morale. Constantly shifting priorities can be demoralizing and disrupt the stable environment we're trying to foster here."

Hannah: "This makes sense, but it's going to be a tough shift. She's used to us agreeing to her needs."

Keisha: "You're right about that. It will be tough, but I think we can work through it if we listen and let her know that we understand her needs. After that, we can expose her to the backlog idea and pitch reviewing it with her to help her understand. In the end, I think she'll welcome it. It will help her understand why things seem to be taking so long from her perspective. And we can work on prioritizing together."

Hannah: "OK, let's take the next step here. Prep an overview of the security issue and how the new ask from Alison delayed that and exposed us. We can use this to demonstrate why we need to prioritize better. Then maybe we can investigate what a centralized managed backlog would look like."

Note Keisha's persistence in addressing Hannah's original reticence to change. Hannah clearly wants things to remain the same and didn't have the data (until now) that illustrates how she just can't keep accepting new work, disrupting her team and sacrificing key work that would harm the organization. With an understanding of what's driving Hannah as an Order Taker, she gently pushes through, attempting to appease her desire for responsiveness and compliance in the face of leadership by suggesting Hannah could better serve Alison by informing her of the impact of her requests. Finally, she connects the dots by telling her how the morale of the team will be served, while establishing a tried-and-true method of managing new requests amidst committed work by pushing the centralized, managed backlog.

Address Team Morale and Stability

It's often been said that employees don't quit bad jobs, they quit bad managers. While the impact to team morale has been instrumental so far in our coping strategies to get The Order Taker manager to empathize and be willing to listen to the need to change their behavior, focusing on the intangibles that are not often thought of in a manager's day to day is equally important. Team morale and the willingness of an employee to derive professional satisfaction and happiness from working for a manager is a valuable, intangible gossamer that is instrumental in achieving a team's objectives and delivering significant positive results to the organization. It's of such importance that organizations often have yearly or even quarterly surveys to measure employee satisfaction and the satisfaction with their managers and organizational leadership. Leaders have learned that talent acquisition and retention are often incredibly expensive. The best leaders know that once talent has been acquired (hired), the best thing they can do is to retain them. However, many managers often lose sight of this impact and fact and The Order Taker is often oblivious to this. Here are some key activities that will elevate this critical, often overlooked element to The Order Taker manager.

Survey the Team: Conduct anonymous surveys to gather honest feedback about the team's morale and the impact of management practices. Present these findings to the manager to underline the emotional and practical repercussions of an interrupt-driven work environment. Don't wait for formal, large cycle, organization-wide satisfaction surveys. Conduct informal, identifiable, and anonymous surveys (perhaps even using a forms technology like Google Forms) to collect and analyze this data using open ended and structured questions. Presenting this to The Order Taker as insights into team satisfaction and retention is the right angle to bolster and reinforce the message of how destabilizing behavior like interruptive order-taking can erode these key pillars of team effectiveness.

Facilitate a Dialogue: Sending these results via email or instant message without a voice track or context can often be more destructive than constructive. In the absence of a contextual narrative, The Order Taker can feel attacked, embarrassed, ashamed, or all of these in combination, thereby establishing an emotional layer of stubborn resistance to change. Instead, begin with a small team leadership meeting of the manager and their immediate direct reports to disclose the collected data. Following this, organize a facilitated session between the manager and the team where employees can express their concerns in a structured manner. This can help the manager hear direct feedback and understand the depth of the team's feelings. In this manner, The Order Taker manager can understand the data associated with their team in a small, privileged setting with context before engaging with the larger team to hear, empathize, and listen.

Putting It Into Practice

As Hannah and Keisha briskly moved through the hallway between meetings, Keisha sensed an opportunity and gently guided Hannah aside.

Keisha: "Listen, Hannah, I've been picking up on a lot of concern from the team about the constant shifts in assignments. It's leading to quite a bit of burnout. Can I talk to you about it quickly? I think I have an idea."

Hannah, always pressed for time, glanced at her watch, but Keisha quickly interjected.

Keisha: "I know you have another meeting, but could you spare just 10 more minutes? I have a proposal that might help us tackle this."

Intrigued and aware of the mounting issues, Hannah nodded, signaling Keisha to continue.

Keisha: "I think we should initiate a listening tour. It's a chance for you to hear directly from the team in a structured yet open setting. I've thought about facilitating some smaller group sessions where you wouldn't just talk but really listen to what the team has to say. They are really struggling with us constantly changing direction and many of them want to understand our true mission and how we'll accomplish meaningful things going forward."

Hannah, usually in the forefront of directing conversations, paused, considering the shift in dynamics Keisha was suggesting.

Hannah: "You mean, I'd just listen? Not solve anything on the spot? We already have all-hands meetings with Q&A segments. Why aren't these issues brought up there?"

Keisha: "Exactly, just listen. The all-hands meetings are great, but they might not provide the safe, intimate space that smaller groups do for everyone to speak up. It's about making the team feel heard in an environment where they're comfortable sharing. We could use an informal survey to kick things off, gather some data-driven feedback, and then engage directly with smaller groups of team members."

Seeing Hannah's hesitance, Keisha added,

Keisha: "Given your role, it might be hard for people to open up in a large group setting. Smaller, manageable groups would encourage more open dialogue where you ask key questions and focus on understanding their concerns. It's a chance to show you're not only approachable but genuinely concerned about their welfare."

Hannah considered the implications, the potential shift in team morale, and the positive impact of being seen as a leader who listens.

Hannah: "Alright. Let's try your way. Set up the first round of sessions. I'll make the time."

Keisha: "Great. I'll organize everything and ensure we have a clear agenda for these sessions. We'll start with gathering the survey data and then move into the listening tour. It's about building a bridge, Hannah, and really tuning into what the team needs to succeed."

Hannah nodded, her mind already racing with the possibilities this
novel approach could unlock.

Hannah: "Thanks, Keisha. I didn't realize how critical this was. Let's
make sure we do this right."

As Keisha watched Hannah head back to her meeting, she felt
a cautious optimism. This was a step toward not only mitigating
the current burnout but also fostering a culture of engagement and
empathy, potentially transforming Hannah's leadership style for the
better.

Promoting Understanding Over Immediate Agreement

Thus far, we've focused on getting The Order Taker manager to
understand the implications of their behavior, when they otherwise
might not have given it a second thought. We provided evidence using
key visuals and data, as well as feedback from the team to help get
them into a position of empathy and willingness to listen. Now, as
an employee of an Order Taker manager, our strategy can shift to
equipping them with a set of tools to help them do what is probably
extremely uncomfortable for them. Pushing back.

The term "pushing back" is controversial and by nature doesn't really
cast the best connotation on partnership formation, but it's important
to recognize a key truth. Push back is part of any healthy partnership
ranging from domestic to professional. If the goal is to establish a
healthy partnership for mutual benefit, one participant in a partnership
cannot simply acquiesce to all demands of the other. There must be a
balance between both. While The Order Taker will be uncomfortable
with this for the abovementioned reasons, giving them the tools to
survive in a healthy partnership is paramount.

Active Listening Techniques: Encourage your manager to adopt
active listening techniques when interacting with leadership,
focusing on understanding the content and context of what is
being communicated before forming a response. This skill can be

enhanced through role-playing exercises or professional development workshops that emphasize listening to comprehend, not
just to reply. By actively listening and then repeating or summarizing what was just said, The Order Taker can gain a clearer
understanding of the demands being made. This process not only
preserves harmony and strengthens rapport but also moderates
their instinct to comply prematurely. Such premature compliance
often stems from their desire to demonstrate teamwork, yet
without full understanding, it can lead to decisions that are not
in the team's (or the organization's) best interest. Active listening
serves as a crucial pause, allowing The Order Taker to consider
the implications of the request and how it aligns with team
goals and resources before agreeing. This deliberate pause helps
prevent the harmful effects of rushed compliance and fosters a
more thoughtful and effective management approach.

Restate and Reflect: Suggest to your manager that you often employ
the "what I hear you saying is" rule to profound effect and suggest
that they might try it at the conclusion of actively listening during
leadership demands. Instead of rushing to accept the demands as
law, to be acted upon as quickly as possible, The Order Taker
pauses, slowing their instincts (already aided by active listening)
and responds to the demand by finishing this sentence.

"What I hear you saying is.…"

In this model, The Order Taker manager restates what has been
articulated without actually agreeing to commit to it. By separating
understanding and commitment, The Order Taker can capture and
understand the orders, but not necessarily commit to the orders. For
the leadership, it truly is a rewarding experience as The Order Taker
manager is actively listening and seeking to understand their requirements and points of view. For the Order Taker manager, it feels
equally rewarding because they are still behaving harmoniously, seeking
understanding and confirmation from leadership of their understanding.
Guide The Order Taker manager to prize hearing the following from the
leadership in that meeting.

THE ORDER TAKER   113

"Yes, that's right."

When The Order Taker hears this, they will have to utilize extraordinary restraint to not accept the tasks. The Order Taker who wants to change must instead seek to conclude the meeting and engage the leadership with a follow-up discussion as to when and how the tasks can be completed against the backlog of existing tasks and priorities. A fully formed example of this in practice is as follows.

"So, what I'm hearing is that you need X done by Y. Let's see how that fits with our current priorities, and I can provide a more detailed timeline by when we meet next."

Putting It Into Practice

Keisha was about to walk into the large conference room for the executive leadership meeting, but she spotted Hannah looking at her phone in a quiet corner of the bustling office hallway just outside.

Keisha: "Hannah, you seem a bit preoccupied. What's on your mind?"

Hannah: "I'm just dreading this upcoming meeting with Alison. She's going to hit me with at least three new requests, and I'm not sure how to handle them without just saying yes to everything. I know if I do the team and our work will be compromised...."

Keisha: "I'm really glad you made that connection and I think it's a great thing. I think we go in and practice active listening. Instead of immediately agreeing, let's take in what she's saying and summarize it, without telling her we'll do it immediately."

Hannah: "You mean, like repeating back what she says to make sure I've got it right?"

Keisha: "Exactly. For instance, you can say, 'What I'm hearing is that you need X, Y, and Z done. Can you confirm that?' This way, you show that you're engaged, and it gives you a moment to process the requests without committing right away."

Hannah: "But what if I'm pressured to agree on the spot? I always feel like I have to give an answer right then."

Keisha was really impressed at how vulnerable Hannah was being in the moment and responded by reassuring her that she had her full support to do the right thing.

Keisha: "How about this. If you feel overwhelmed, turn to me and I'll help by summarizing the discussion and explaining that we need to assess how these new tasks align with our current priorities. I can be the 'bad guy' who says we'll get back to her with a structured plan."

Hannah: "I don't know Keisha ... that might look like I'm not in control."

Keisha: "Not at all. It actually shows that you're being thorough and considering all factors before making a decision. It's about strategic leadership, not just quick answers. Plus, it positions you as someone who values thoughtful planning."

Hannah: "It might actually give me the space I need to think things through and not just react in the moment."

Keisha: "Right. And it's important that this doesn't come off as stalling. It's about being responsible and making sure we're committing to what we can actually deliver. It's managing expectations."

Hannah: "Okay, let's try it. I'm not used to pushing back, but I trust this approach might help change the dynamic for the better."

Keisha: "I'll be right there with you. After the meeting, we can debrief and plan out how to handle the requests in a way that makes sense for our team's workload and goals."

Hannah: "Thanks, Keisha. I really appreciate the support. Let's see how this goes."

This dialogue illustrates a strategic approach to handling overwhelming demands by utilizing active listening and thoughtful communication. By incorporating Keisha's advice, Hannah is equipped to navigate the meeting more effectively, demonstrating leadership that balances immediate responsiveness with careful consideration of long-term team capacity and strategic alignment.

Provide "Outs" for Strategic Prioritization

Providing an "out" for The Order Taker manager is equivalent to helping them develop a set of coping mechanisms to harmoniously leave a leadership meeting where demands have been articulated without feeling the need to immediately agree and accept them. If you can help equip your manager with these tactics, which ultimately are equivalent to key responses to conclude a demanding leadership meeting by focusing on understanding the requirement and capturing it, it will help The Order Taker evolve.

> **Backlog Management:** The concept of a backlog can take many forms. In many organizations, the backlog is the list of programs, projects, and tasks that teams must complete to deliver value back to the organization. Whether it exists formally or informally, the first step is to write it down. Informal or ethereal backlogs without evidence of Who, What, When, Where, Why, and How often lead to a set of disasters that extend beyond the impact of order-taking. Write down the backlog and share it with your manager, often reviewing it and preparing an executive leadership view of the backlog to articulate timelines, effort, and projected impact. Acquire commitment from your manager that all new requests get added to the backlog and then are triaged accordingly before any work is to begin. This helps in setting realistic expectations with stakeholders and provides a structured way to deal with requests. It also insulates what could be perceived as interrupting priorities from management from employees who are already working on committed tasks.

> **Scripted Responses:** Equip the manager with phrases that offer a way to defer immediate commitments, such as the following responses. Obviously, we don't want our manager reading verbatim from a list of perceived excuses, but generally providing some of these techniques can help The Order Taker arrest their compliance instinct and navigate a successful conclusion to active listening.

"I understand the importance of this. Let me review our current projects to see how we can best allocate resources to address this effectively."

"I think I have a good understanding of the requirements now. I'll add this to our backlog and being triaging this immediately and report back on where we think we can fit it in."

"These requirements make a lot of sense and are extremely innovative and transformative. I know that my team would really like to work on this. I'll begin a swift prioritization exercise and get back to you and let you know what we recommend to get this going as soon as possible."

"The team, as you know, is extremely utilized on existing commitments. With these new demands, I can come back to you with a recommendation on what would happen if we prioritized these new needs over existing projects."

Note how these not only are semiharmonious responses to leadership but also simultaneously communicate to leadership that there are competing priorities that must be weighed. This is in stark contrast to simply accepting the new demands wholesale and not educating leadership on the true implications of what they asked for. For the manager, it communicates to leadership that they are balancing existing commitments to organizational success and new initiatives and ideas that will make a transformational impact on the organization. Also, for The Order Taker, it helps insulate their team against interrupt-driven new projects and it helps them systematically accept new requirements without jeopardizing their team's success.

Putting It Into Practice

For this section, let's assume that Keisha has successfully convinced Hannah of the detrimental effects of her order-taking behavior. Based on her willingness to form a stable partnership with her leadership, Hannah is workshopping some key phrases she can use to indicate that she understands the new requirements from leadership, without committing to them and assuming that they are indeed orders that need to be immediately filled.

Hannah can use the following responses as inspiration to effectively communicate her understanding of leadership's demands while emphasizing the need for careful prioritization and planning. Note that no one should seek to memorize these word for word. However, using the gist of these recommended responses, The Order Taker manager can have a natural conversation where understanding is communicated, followed by transparent prioritization.

1. "I see the potential impact of these new requirements. Let me assess our ongoing projects to understand where we can integrate this most effectively without compromising our current deliverables. I'll schedule a prioritization meeting to discuss this further."

2. "Thank you for bringing this to my attention. I will review our team's current workload and get back to you with a strategic plan on how we can accommodate this new project."

3. "These are certainly transformative ideas that align well with our long-term goals. I'll add them to our project backlog and propose a few scenarios on how we might prioritize these effectively during our next leadership review session."

4. "I appreciate your input and see the urgency here. Let me consult with the team and evaluate our current timelines. I'll organize a meeting with you and other key stakeholders to ensure we align our priorities with organizational objectives."

5. "This initiative sounds exciting and beneficial. To ensure we handle this properly, I'll need to analyze our resources and existing commitments. Expect a follow-up from me next week where we can set some concrete steps forward."

6. "Your proposal is compelling, and I understand why we should prioritize it. Allow me some time to review our current projects so I can provide a realistic timeline and resource allocation plan. We can then review these details together and make an informed decision."

7. "It's clear that this project could have significant benefits. I'll initiate a prioritization exercise with my team and set up a time

for us to go over these plans together. Your insights during this meeting would be invaluable to ensure we're making the best strategic decisions."

8. "Given the potential of what you're proposing, I want to ensure we approach this with the diligence it deserves. I will prepare an impact analysis and a proposal for integration with our current projects. Let's plan to discuss this at the next leadership meeting."

Each of these responses helps Hannah articulate that she is attentive to the needs of leadership while also responsible for the management of her team's workload and the organization's overall strategic direction. This approach not only communicates the need for thoughtful consideration of new projects but also sets the stage for more collaborative and transparent decision-making processes.

Summing It Up

In navigating the complexities of leadership within a fast-paced corporate environment, the archetype of the Order Taker presents both challenges and opportunities for organizational growth and personal development. The Order Taker is often characterized by their swift compliance to executive demands, prioritizing immediate responses over strategic evaluation. This behavior, while seemingly beneficial in making the team appear responsive to leadership demands, often leads to disruptions in planned projects, strains on resources, and a negative impact on team morale and performance. Additionally, the constant focus shift can leave projects abandoned, hurting the organization.

1. **Understanding the Impact:** The Order Taker must recognize the broader consequences of their actions on the team's productivity and well-being. Continuously accepting and implementing new orders without proper assessment can lead to project delays, unfinished tasks, and potential risks that could have been mitigated with a more measured approach.

2. **Strategic Prioritization:** Implementing a system where incoming tasks are assessed and prioritized can significantly alleviate the pressure on the team. This involves setting up structured prioritization meetings that include key stakeholders to ensure that decisions are made with a clear understanding of current workloads and strategic goals.

3. **Communication Is Key:** Developing effective communication strategies is crucial. The Order Taker should practice articulating the need for balance between new initiatives and ongoing projects to the leadership. Using scripted responses as inspiration, The Order Taker can defer immediate compliance for strategic assessment, which is crucial in maintaining this balance.

4. **Fostering Team Morale:** Regular feedback mechanisms, such as surveys and open discussions, can help The Order Taker gauge team morale and gather insights into the emotional and practical impacts of their management style. Understanding these can guide the Order Taker to adjust their approach and improve team satisfaction and retention.

5. **Leadership Development:** The Order Taker should focus on developing leadership skills that extend beyond compliance. This includes training on strategic thinking, risk assessment, and resource management. Leadership development programs and mentoring can provide the necessary tools and insights.

6. **Empathetic Leadership:** Incorporating empathy into their leadership style can transform an Order Taker from a mere implementer of orders into a visionary leader who values team input and understands the importance of balanced workload management. This shift can significantly enhance team dynamics and organizational output.

By addressing these key areas, The Order Taker can evolve into a strategic leader who not only responds to immediate demands but also anticipates future challenges and aligns team efforts with organizational objectives. This transformation is essential for sustaining long-term growth and maintaining a competitive edge in the dynamic corporate landscape.

For employees working under an Order Taker, influencing a shift from instinctive compliance to strategic partnership involves tactfully challenging the manager's impulse to immediately respond to executive demands. This task isn't easy, as it requires subverting The Order Taker's need to appear harmonious and responsive. Employees can aid in this transformation by emphasizing the long-term benefits of measured responses and collaborative decision-making. They can contribute by communicating the impacts of abrupt project shifts on both outcomes and team morale, advocating for strategy meetings where priorities are collaboratively assessed, and participating in feedback mechanisms that highlight the effects of current management practices. By presenting these insights constructively, employees can foster an environment where reflective leadership is valued over reactive management, promoting a culture of strategic thinking and enhancing team effectiveness and satisfaction.

CHAPTER 7

The Raw Nerve

Background

In the high-stakes environment of organizational strategy, where millions hinge on the right technological foundation, Sam, the managing vice president of the organization's technology team, finds herself at a pivotal juncture. Tasked with a monumental decision—to choose a data and analytics platform that will underpin the organization's entire analytical reporting capabilities—she feels the weight of urgency pressed upon her by Alison, the chief data officer and the senior leadership team. This decision is not just crucial; it's transformational, with the company set to invest millions in the chosen solution.

Over the past several months, Sam's team of vice presidents and their teams, led by the meticulous and thorough Omar, has been deeply engaged in a rigorous evaluation process. They've conducted extensive research, orchestrated detailed proof-of-concept exercises, and thoroughly compared the offerings of two leading vendors. Their approach has been methodically data-driven, aiming to culminate in a well-founded recommendation that would ensure the organization's future analytical prowess.

However, as the predictable timeline to reach a conclusive recommendation draws closer, in a crucial Zoom meeting, Sam's characteristic impatience as a Raw Nerve archetype surfaces with a jarring display of urgency. Under intense pressure from Alison and other executives to expedite the decision, Sam grasps at a piece of information she encountered—a recent news report criticizing one vendor for customer satisfaction issues. Seizing this anecdote as a decisive factor, she abruptly discounts the comprehensive eight-week evaluation process that Omar and his team have been painstakingly leading.

"I think we've seen enough to make a decision," Sam asserts abruptly in the meeting, her tone leaving little room for debate. "The risks with the first technology solution, considering the customer satisfaction issues reported recently in the news, make it too big a gamble. I think we go ahead with the second choice."

Omar, who has been coordinating the evaluation process, is left aghast. Months of diligent work—countless hours spent in analysis, discussions, and validations—seem disregarded in a moment of impulsive judgment. The depth and rigor of their investigation, designed to parse through technical capabilities, cost implications, and strategic fit, are suddenly overshadowed by a single piece of external news that may not even bear relevance to their specific needs or context.

"This decision isn't just about reacting to a headline," Omar tries to interject, hoping to stem the rush to judgment. "Our teams have been working to ensure that our choice is backed by solid data and aligns with our strategic goals. We still need to complete our final assessments to truly understand which platform aligns best with our long-term objectives."

Despite Omar's protest, Sam moves ahead with her gut instinct, electing to deliver her recommendation to Alison and leadership. In fact, the more that Omar attempts to make her see the implications of utilizing a careful data-driven evaluation framework for such an enormous choice, the more she reacts with annoyance, impatience, and anger. Her decision reflects the quintessential Raw Nerve reaction—swift, driven by surface stimuli, and laden with potential strategic missteps. This impetuous move not only undermines the extensive preparatory work done by her team but also risks locking the organization into a platform choice that might not serve its intended purpose, based solely on an anecdote that lacks comprehensive validation.

As the meeting concludes, Omar is left contemplating the repercussions of this abrupt decision—how it might affect team morale, the trust placed in the investigative process, and ultimately, the organization's ability to leverage its data for competitive advantage. He is a volatile mixture of frustration and dumbfounded disbelief that anyone could make such a critical decision based on whispers on the internet, and overall frustration that he and his team wasted their time. This scenario starkly highlights the challenges of working under a Raw Nerve leader whose instinctive reactions can sometimes lead to profound strategic oversights, jeopardizing long-term success for the sake of immediate resolution.

The Archetype Defined

In the high-stakes theater of modern organizations, where decisions must often be made rapidly and under pressure, The Raw Nerve archetype emerges as a notably volatile and unpredictable player. This type of manager is characterized by a propensity for knee-jerk reactions to challenges and an emotional volatility that permeates their leadership style. Originating from a blend of high personal standards and a fiercely competitive nature, The Raw Nerve is both a catalyst for action and a potential source of workplace turbulence.

The Raw Nerve typically develops in environments where quick decision-making is prized over deliberate thought. Often, these managers have ascended through the ranks in industries that value speed and results more than anything else, such as start-ups, high-growth tech companies, or any field undergoing rapid change. This background reinforces a mindset in The Raw Nerve manager archetype that equates immediate action with effectiveness, often at the expense of thoroughness or the well-being of team members. Their firm belief is that there is always an invisible clock ticking down the seconds they have to make decisions and that any action, if it's based on instinctive experience, is valuable.

A hallmark of The Raw Nerve's management style is a high emotional reactivity, which can manifest as snap judgments or abrupt changes in business direction. This reactivity is frequently compounded by a lack of emotional regulation, making The Raw Nerve seem unpredictable or overly aggressive. While this can lead to a dynamic, yet unstable, work environment, it often results in strategic missteps and a team culture riddled with anxiety. A study by Sy, T. et al., published in the *Journal of Applied Psychology*, reveals that a leader's emotional mood significantly impacts the mood of group members and the overall affective tone within the team.[*] In other words, when a manager exhibits emotional volatility, including snap judgments and directions, it can create a contagious effect, influencing the emotional climate of the entire group. This has implications for team collaboration, trust, and overall organizational dynamics.

The influence of a Raw Nerve manager on a team can be profound and double-edged. On one hand, their ability to make swift decisions can lead to impressive short-term achievements and the quick pivoting that is sometimes necessary in reactive business situations. On the other hand, their impulsive nature can disrupt team cohesion, undermine long-term planning, and lead to a high turnover rate. The emotional toll on employees can be significant, as team members might constantly feel on edge, trying to anticipate and adapt to the manager's unpredictable demands. For employees, each interaction, each meeting where well-thought-out approaches to challenges or problems can be a puzzling, anxiety-inducing experience in which they often wonder "which version of my boss will I get in this meeting?"

For The Raw Nerve to adapt more successfully to the demands of leadership, they must learn to temper their impulsiveness with strategic thinking. Embracing methods that foster emotional intelligence, such as mindfulness and stress management techniques, can be beneficial. Furthermore, developing a more inclusive decision-making process that involves gathering input from diverse team members can help mitigate the risks associated with hasty decisions. As employees working under such a manager, the difficult part will be to attempt to coach your manager along these paths to mitigate the negative outcomes a Raw Nerve archetype can bring about.

While The Raw Nerve archetype brings a unique energy and decisiveness to leadership, their effectiveness is often hampered by their impetuous nature. By recognizing the limitations of their style and encouraging the adoption of a more balanced approach to decision-making, Raw Nerve managers can evolve into leaders who not only

[*] T. Sy, S. Côté, and R. Saavedra, 2005, "The Contagious Leader: Impact of the Leader's Mood on the Mood of Group Members, Group Affective Tone, and Group Processes," *Journal of Applied Psychology* 90(2): 295–305, DOI: 10.1037/0021-9010.90.2.295.

inspire action but also nurture stable and productive team environments.

Coping Strategies

Working under a Raw Nerve manager, characterized by impulsiveness and emotional decision-making, can often leave employees feeling unsettled and frustrated. However, there are effective strategies that can help mitigate these challenges, ensuring that your work environment remains productive, and your professional integrity stays intact. The following are some prioritized coping strategies.

Build Resilience and Support Networks

Navigating the workplace under a Raw Nerve manager necessitates the construction of robust support networks that extend beyond your immediate team. This strategy involves forming alliances with a diverse group of influential stakeholders, including skip-level managers, peers of your manager, and key executive stakeholders involved in critical projects and decisions. These connections are invaluable for creating a chorus of well-informed, impactful individuals who can understand and potentially influence the outcomes of your manager's instinctive reactions.

>   **Engage Broadly but Carefully:** Begin by fostering relationships with individuals both inside and outside of your immediate team who are positioned at various levels within the organization. This includes reaching out to skip-level managers and peers of your manager, not with the intent of complaining, but rather to discuss project progress, share insights, and subtly highlight the risks associated with decision-making that lacks data-backed research. Focus on those that have a stake in the particular project or initiative and engage them in an information-sharing status update where you carefully weave in the specifics of the project and decision in question. As you do this, realize that anything you say or write will probably make it back to your immediate

manager, so engage carefully with full knowledge that your efforts will likely be seen by your Raw Nerve boss. If done correctly, you can make the communication innocuous enough that it will probably be seen by your manager as stakeholder management. Make it such that your core considerations are communicated through one-on-one verbal communication with these individuals.

Actively Recruit and Engage Stakeholders: Use these interactions to educate your broader network about the nuances of projects under your manager's control and why measured approaches utilizing data and strategy are preferred over instinctive, "raw nerve" reactions. Discuss the potential impacts of decisions driven by gut reactions rather than thorough analysis carefully. Verbally engage with these stakeholders, peers, and skip-level managers, and frame the conversations around seeking advice or brainstorming solutions to avert a rushed decision rather than directly challenging your manager's approach. Finally, encourage and invite these stakeholders to take an active interest in the ongoing projects and decisions. Their increased awareness can lead to more oversight, which might temper impulsive decisions by introducing more checks and balances into the process.

- Incorporate insights from external mentors and industry peers to bring diverse perspectives into your strategic network. These perspectives can be invaluable during internal discussions, offering alternative solutions or highlighting best practices that can inform and improve your manager's decision-making process. Promote the value of consulting with external advisers, engaging with vendors, and interacting with industry peers to The Raw Nerve manager as a significant benefit to the decision-making process. This approach should be presented before any critical decisions where there's a risk that they might make a hasty, emotionally driven choice.

Cultivate Your Influence and Bring Them Along: As your relationships develop, you'll naturally begin to influence the broader dialogue around decision-making processes within your organization. This influence should be wielded carefully and always with the goal of advancing project goals and organizational objectives. It should never be used to diminish, marginalize, or sideline your Raw Nerve manager. Remember, the goal is to coach, develop, and manage upward, bringing your Raw Nerve manager along, rather than seek to go around them, which never works well in the long term. Instead, as your influence grows, seek to bring your manager into the conversation, demonstrating why the rest of the organization values this approach and help them see how they can take part in this process.

By expanding your support network to include a wider range of influential individuals within the organization, you create an environment where quick, unvetted decisions are more likely to be questioned and refined by others instead of just you, or your immediate peers under The Raw Nerve manager. This not only helps in moderating the impact of a Raw Nerve manager's impulsive decisions but also contributes to a more deliberative, data-driven approach to leadership within your team.

Putting It Into Practice

Omar finds himself in a precarious position. A decision looms over the selection of a data analytics platform that could dictate the future operational landscape of the company. Sam, under the pressing influence of Alison and the leadership team, appears poised to make a swift and seemingly arbitrary decision on the matter. This decision, based more on external pressure than on the meticulous months-long evaluation process Omar's team has undertaken, threatens to lock the company into a potentially ill-suited platform.

Flabbergasted by Sam's approach but acutely aware of the need to navigate this situation delicately, Omar opts for an immediate but cautious strategy. He chooses instant messaging as his communication tool with Terry—a managing vice president of a line of business division and a peer to Sam. This medium allows for rapid engagement and the swift intervention that the situation demands. Omar is conscious that anything he communicates could potentially circulate back to Sam, so he carefully crafts his messages to express concern without overtly criticizing Sam's decision-making style. His goal is to ensure that the decision is revisited with the comprehensive data his team has been gathering, thereby safeguarding the company from potential strategic missteps.

The conversation needs to be both urgent and tactful, balancing the immediate need to address the situation with the long-term relationships and dynamics within the executive team. Omar's approach demonstrates his strategic acumen and his commitment to the organization's well-being, navigating the fine line between proactive engagement and respectful communication. See the following conversation:

Omar: Hi Terry, hope you're well. Have you got a minute?

Terry: Hey Omar, sure, what's up? On a Zoom meeting in listen-only mode.…

Omar: I'm reaching out because we're nearing a critical decision on the data analytics platform, and there's a strong push from Alison to expedite this. Sam is leaning toward making an early call based on some preliminary feedback, but we're not done with our comprehensive evaluation yet and I want to get her and you the data to make an informed decision.

Terry: I heard about that. Isn't the evaluation supposed to run for another month?

Omar: Exactly, we've scheduled four more weeks to ensure that we cover all bases. The team's working through some crucial assessments. I'm afraid jumping the gun could lead us to choose a platform that might not align with our long-term needs.

Terry: That sounds risky, especially since it could directly impact my division too. Making the wrong choice could make my life VERY difficult. What are your concerns?

Omar: Well, my main worry is that a hasty decision could lock us into a technology that's cumbersome and limits your team's productivity. From what we've seen, one of the platforms has significant integration and usability issues, which would be a nightmare for your operations.

Terry: That's alarming, indeed. We can't afford setbacks like that. What do you suggest?

Omar: I think getting your viewpoint on this is going to be extremely valuable. I was hoping you could weigh in with your perspective on making sure we give the data a chance to help us make the choice, given your team's stake in this. I'd also like to set up a Zoom meeting where I can walk you through the data we've gathered so far and discuss Sam's leaning. Your input would be invaluable before this goes any further.

Terry: I appreciate you bringing this to me, Omar. Let's definitely schedule that. It's crucial we make an informed decision that doesn't just react to pressure but considers the implications for everyone involved.

Omar: Thanks, Terry. I'll send over some available times. Looking forward to your insights, and really appreciate your support on navigating this. I'll let Sam know that we're going to connect on this as well so she's aware.

Terry: No problem, Omar. It's important we get this right. Talk soon.

Note how Omar has identified Terry as a stakeholder who could benefit or be negatively impacted by this decision. It's a great choice as he's a direct peer of Sam's in the organization and his feedback and questions might be the right type of influence to slow down Sam's reactive decision and recommendation. Omar engages Terry from a position of seeking advice and articulates "worry" instead of leveling judgments, frustrations, and incriminations of Sam's Raw Nerve reaction to pressure. Of significant note is how Omar realizes that anything he says will most likely get back to Sam, so he makes sure that if she were to read this thread herself, she would not take offense. In fact, notice how Omar makes sure he tells Terry that he's going to take it a step further by informing Sam of their upcoming meeting together to discuss the data. Finally, notice how Omar gets a meeting with Terry where he can verbally articulate with more nuance Sam's gut reaction and make recommendations how they can countermand the impulsive decision without a written paper trail.

Such a response isn't most people's first reaction. Omar had to spend a lot of time navigating his own emotions, let alone the disbelief in Sam's reactionary, imprecise and impetuous decision-making in order to arrive at an approach so nuanced and balanced. It undoubtedly took him a lot of time to go through this process, especially if this had been his first encounter with this management archetype. For those of us with experience in working for a Raw Nerve manager, this transition to a delicate coping strategy occurs faster.

Focus on Getting Delegation Buy-In

Empowering yourself and your team can significantly buffer the impacts of a Raw Nerve's impulsive decisions. Advocate for clear delegation of responsibilities, where you and your team have the autonomy to make decisions within a defined scope. This approach not only builds trust but also enhances team morale and engagement by reducing the direct impact of hasty decisions made by your manager. It allows for a sense of control over your work, fostering a proactive rather than reactive workplace culture. The caveat of course, is that once this autonomy has been sanctioned and agreed to by The Raw Nerve manager, you will undoubtedly have to judiciously remind your boss that you are in fact in charge of the outcomes and that any reaction from them is not only undesirable but also detrimental to the organization, the team, and the decisions or outcomes. In other words, be cautious as while getting delegation buy in from The Raw Nerve manager is typically not challenging, the difficulty is in ensuring that in the heat of the moment, The Raw Nerve respects the previously agreed-to delegation arrangement. To help with this empowerment, make sure that you do the following.

Secure Written Decision-Making Process Commitments: Request or write documented agreements or project charters that outline the decision-making process, including timelines for evaluations, deliverables, and final decisions. This formalizes the manager's commitment to depend on detailed groundwork laid by the team, and not just on their instincts. Having this in writing adds a layer of accountability, providing a reference point, should the need arise to remind the manager of agreed-upon processes.

Acquire Frequent Verbal Reassurances: During meetings, or one-on-one sessions, seek verbal affirmations from the manager acknowledging the team's expertise and the critical nature of the established timelines as a function of the agreed-upon decision-making process. This could be facilitated through regular update sessions where the manager is encouraged by their team to publicly back the team's recommendations and timelines, reinforcing their support and reliance on the team's systematic approach to decision-making.

Make the Process Transparent: Enhance transparency by involving the manager in the process early on. Schedule regular briefing sessions where the team can present findings, progress, and potential risks associated with the project. This involvement not only keeps the manager informed but also builds their trust in the team's capabilities, making them more likely to adhere to the planned timelines and rely on the team's expertise. Line these interactions with the importance of how following the process to completion is preferable to taking shortcuts and making gut reaction or instinctive decisions. This can preemptively help The Raw Nerve manager arrest their own instinctive reactions when the pressure is on.

Putting It Into Practice

In a pivotal meeting with Terry and Sam, Omar successfully leveraged Terry's supportive stance to sway Sam toward allowing the team ample time to complete their thorough evaluation of the analytics platforms. Terry, understanding the strategic implications of the decision, offered to join Sam in advocating for additional time to Alison, should the need arise to further justify the extended timeline. This collaborative approach underscored the importance of a data-driven decision-making process. By the meeting's conclusion, Sam, influenced by the united front presented by Omar and Terry, consented to let the team finalize their assessment, ensuring that the final recommendation would be robust and substantiated by empirical data. This agreement marks a significant step toward optimizing the decision-making process, reinforcing a commitment to strategic thoroughness and precision. Following the guidance, Omar documents the agreement reached and the outcome of the session and plans to follow up with verbal reinforcement to manage Sam's Raw Nerve instincts as they execute the remainder of the process.

To: Sam

Subject: Update and Appreciation for Strategic Support on Platform Evaluation

CC: Terry, Project Evaluation Team

Hi Sam,

Thank you for entrusting us with the analytics platform evaluation. I appreciate your strategic approach to hold off on final decisions until we've thoroughly analyzed all data.

> Note that in this sentence Omar is expressing the desired behavior he wants Sam to adopt and grow into, effectively thanking her in advance for arresting her Raw Nerve instincts.

I'm also grateful that both you and Terry fully support our commitment to a data-driven conclusion, reinforcing the importance of our meticulous process.

> Here Omar gently reminds Sam that it's not just her reactionary instincts here that matter, but Terry effectively as their customer (who will be impacted by this choice greatly) is expecting the successful conclusion of this data-driven exercise to avoid gut instinct reactions that might result in the wrong choice.

I'm preparing to present our findings and recommendations to the executive team. I'll share these with you first to ensure alignment and that there are no surprises.

Here Omar is adhering to some basic advice that all professionals need to follow. Never surprise your manager. His plan to present Sam the findings before anyone else, allow her to react, for him to manage those reactions and then to present it to the larger team as a unified front, instead of her reacting emotionally and doing damage during the leadership presentation. He's effectively anticipating The Raw Nerve behavior and mitigating it in advance.

Your decision to empower our team to lead this evaluation showcases exceptional leadership, especially under the usual pressures for quick decisions. It's reassuring to have your support, allowing us to deliver well-founded recommendations that will benefit our long-term goals.

Note how Omar finally engages in rewarding, reinforcement behavior, effectively using gratitude to reinforce Sam's positive move ment away from her initial gut reaction to more strategic thinking that shows confidence in the team that has done all the work so far. This effectively repairs Sam's instinctive "bombshell" reaction from before and sets everyone on the path to using data to make the decision.

Best regards,
Omar

One final observation is how succinct and executive level this communication is. It likely fits on a phone screen without excessive scrolling, has plenty of whitespace with paragraph breaks and is direct and meaningful.

Use Escalation Wisely and Diplomatically

Escalation, often misconstrued as simply bypassing one's immediate supervisor to seek resolution from higher-ups, is more nuanced and strategic, particularly when managing the challenges associated with a Raw Nerve manager. This type of escalation involves building a coalition of like-minded colleagues and stakeholders who share a concern about the potential impacts of impulsive decision-making on the team's objectives and the organization's broader goals.

In practice, this approach is about aligning with others (without complaining about The Raw Nerve manager, or hurling accusations) who understand the necessity of a balanced and thoughtful decision-making process and can collectively influence The Raw Nerve manager. By pooling insights and concerns, this group can present a united front, providing a broader perspective that may help temper the manager's instinctive reactions. This method of escalation does not directly challenge authority but instead seeks to enrich the decision-making process with diverse inputs and collaborative reflection. This is reflected before in Omar's instant message conversation with Terry as he seeks to build such a coalition.

However, there may come a time when engaging The Raw Nerve manager's direct supervisor is going to be required. Despite all the coping strategies, if employees can't restrain or reign in The Raw Nerve manager, direct institutional authority may be required. In this situation, which is in line with the traditional definition of escalation, one must exercise extreme caution and patience. Every employee should make a habit of having a recurring skip-level one-on-one meeting series with their manager's manager. These meetings should be topical, have an agenda or central topic, and be wisely utilized. When seeking to involve the skip-level manager to mitigate The Raw Nerve, the same strategy should apply as when building a coalition. The following are some Do's and Don'ts for escalation.

Do's

- Process the difficult emotions and frustrations ahead of the meeting so they don't "leak" into the conversation and affect your desired goals and outcomes.
- Ask questions that you already know the answer to, under the guise of seeking advice and input.
  - (e.g., "I'm assuming that someone of your experience values purposeful, data-driven decision-making, so I'm interested to see if you think my approach to solving this issue is on the right track.")

- Seek, as the primary outcome, a response reinforcing your suggestions to "right-track" the decision-making process.
  - (e.g., "Yes, that's right Omar. I think executing the process to completion is wise to make sure we don't overlook anything.")
- Include who you've spoken to that already agrees with you about your approach to solving the impact of The Raw Nerve manager's reactionary decision.

Describe how you plan to roll it back without directly challenging The Raw Nerve manager or impugning their authority but making them part of the process of right-tracking.

Don'ts

- Make accusations, incriminate The Raw Nerve manager, or describe how detrimental the person is to the organization no matter how true it is.
- Talk directly about The Raw Nerve manager's undesirable traits, choices, and decisions directly.
- Complain or make incriminations about the catastrophic impact of The Raw Nerve manager's decisions or behaviors (currently or historically).
- Go into the meeting without a recommendation of what to do (never go to any manager with a problem without a solution).

Approaching escalation in this way helps to preserve professional relationships and organizational harmony. It avoids the appearance of subversion or personal grievance, framing the initiative as a constructive effort to enhance outcomes for everyone involved. This careful, considered approach to escalation ensures that it is viewed as a responsible and necessary measure for organizational well-being rather than a confrontational move, making it more likely to be received positively and lead to effective change.

Knowing when and how to escalate issues is critical when dealing with a manager whose decision-making could jeopardize team objectives or the broader organizational goals. Escalation should not be your first response but reserved for situations where internal strategies have failed to mitigate the risk posed by impulsive managerial decisions. It is vital to approach escalation judiciously, ensuring that you have documented evidence and a clear rationale for why intervention is needed. This helps in maintaining professional integrity and ensures that the escalation is seen as constructive rather than confrontational.

Putting It Into Practice

Despite receiving written affirmations to follow a thorough, data-driven approach, Sam's impatience is growing, and signs indicate that she may soon double down on her initial, instinctive decision regarding the data analytics platform. Sensing the urgency and the potential repercussions of such a premature decision, Omar discussed the matter with Terry, who is deeply invested in the outcome as a primary user of the platform. Recognizing the gravity of the situation and the need for additional oversight, they both agreed that involving Haruto, Sam's manager, could be crucial in moderating the decision process. Seeking Haruto's support to ensure that all due diligence is observed before any final decision is communicated became imperative. The following conversation unfolds as Omar engages in a regularly scheduled skip-level manager meeting over Zoom with Haruto, aiming to secure his backing and potentially temper Sam's rush toward an unsubstantiated choice.

> **Omar:** "Hi Haruto, I hope you're doing well today. I wanted to discuss our approach to finalizing the data analytics platform decision. As you know, Sam has been leaning toward making an early call based on some initial feedback, and we're still wrapping up our comprehensive evaluation."
>
> **Haruto:** "Hello Omar, yes, I'm aware of the situation. It's crucial we get this right, given the investment and the impact it will have across the company."
>
> **Omar:** "Great. I've been in talks with Terry, whose division will be one of the primary users of the platform. He strongly supports waiting for the complete results of our evaluation process before

making a final decision. He believes that the data-driven approach will ensure we choose the most capable platform for our needs."

Haruto: "That makes sense. It's good to hear that Terry is on board. How close are we to completing the evaluation?"

Omar: "We are just a few weeks away from wrapping everything up. All that remains are some critical areas of investigation that could significantly influence our choice. Given the magnitude of this decision, Terry and I feel it would be prudent to ensure our final recommendation is as informed as possible."

Haruto: "Absolutely, the last thing we want is to rush this decision and regret it later. Do you need anything to support this?"

Omar: "I think it would be great if you and Sam could help facilitate a session to review the recommendation as we communicate it to Alison and the wider leadership team. Obviously, we'd share the recommendation with Sam and you first. While Sam has already hinted at a preference, we believe it's crucial that this preference is backed by the complete set of data and evaluations. I'm hoping to count on your support to ensure this session takes place. Do you think we're still on the right track?"

Haruto: "Yes, I see the wisdom in that. It's important that any decision of this scale is fully vetted. I'll speak with Sam about arranging this session. You're absolutely on the right track here, Omar. Ensuring that our decision is data-driven and comprehensive will safeguard our interests and maximize the platform's benefits."

Omar: "Thanks, Haruto. I appreciate your understanding and support. Ensuring we have comprehensive data to back our choice will definitely help mitigate risks and align with our strategic goals. I'll keep you updated on our progress and will coordinate with you and Sam on setting up the review session."

Haruto: "Thanks, Omar. Keep up the great work, and let's make sure we get this right. Looking forward to seeing the final analysis and moving forward with the best option."

Omar: "Will do, Haruto. Thanks again for your time and support today. I'll be in touch soon."

In this conversation, Omar effectively uses the strategy of engaging higher management to ensure that the decision-making process remains thorough, and data-driven. By confirming support from another key stakeholder (Terry) and respectfully seeking to align Sam's early (Raw Nerve-based) decision with comprehensive data, Omar helps steer the project toward a more deliberate and informed conclusion, keeping in line with best practices for handling a potentially impulsive managerial style.

Document and Record "Drift"

There will undoubtedly be times where the previous coping strategies will not be sufficient to manage the outcomes of The Raw Nerve manager. In each of the abovementioned coping strategies, and throughout this book, it's conceivable that they simply don't have the desired effect and you're going to be left with the aftermath of being unable to arrest your manager's difficult behaviors. For The Raw Nerve, this means that if you're unable to avert disaster by influencing, escalating, and managing upward, you're going to have to find a way to publish your own recommendations after a reactive or instinctive decision has already been made.

Meticulous documentation and record-keeping are your best defense against the fallout from impulsive decisions. Keeping detailed records of decisions, rationales, and outcomes not only provides a basis for future reference but also protects the team during accountability checks. This strategy is particularly important in environments where decisions are frequently made under pressure and without full consideration of their long-term impacts. Documentation can also support your arguments during discussions or escalations, providing unmistakable evidence for alternative strategies or the reconsideration of decisions.

Publish the Data and Distribute Broadly: Even after the decision has been made and The Raw Nerve's instinctive behavior reigns supreme, or the gut reaction's outcomes are irreversible in the short term, if you can complete the process to drive data insights around the choice, make an effort to still publish the outcome widely to your assembled influencers and communities. Clear it with your manager so they are not surprised that your data and findings conflict with their gut reaction. In this scenario, describe how the data tells a slightly different story than the decision that was made, but you feel that publishing it will help the organization at large understand the implications of the choice.

Be Diplomatic in the Distribution: It's easy to sting with the inability to subvert the gut reaction, but publishing the data and recommendation after the fact should not be a revenge tour, nor should it be a "see, I told you so" exercise when the implications of the gut reaction from The Raw Nerve manager are realized in the future (as good as that probably would feel). It should be expressed as an accountability measure, and a demonstration of the practice that the organization should formalize prior to making choices. By demonstrating good behavior by publishing it without impugning anyone, you can utilize it as a platform to illustrate how the organization should make decisions moving forward.

Implementing these strategies requires patience and a strategic approach to influence change gradually. Each step taken to fortify your position and that of your team contributes to a more stable and less volatile work environment. While working under a Raw Nerve manager will always present unique challenges, these strategies provide a framework for navigating these difficulties with confidence and professionalism.

Putting It Into Practice

Omar connects with Sam on Slack to try to influence her to make a data-driven decision, rather than an instinctive one. He senses it coming so he tries to appeal to her before the critical moment where she commits the organization to a precarious path.

Omar: Hi Sam, I hope you're having a great morning. I wanted to touch base with you regarding our upcoming decision on our new collaboration platform adoption.

Sam: Hi Omar, yes, as usual, Alison is breathing down our necks, so I am going to recommend we go ahead with the contract. I read some good things in the news about the company yesterday, so I think we can trust them.

Omar: What else is new right? I do think we want to make sure we don't repeat our path with the data platform adoption where we moved ahead without fully evaluating our comprehensive findings. We faced some significant challenges postdecision that could have easily been mitigated if we took the time to complete our due diligence before deciding. The data-driven findings the team published about the data platform clearly articulate how if we considered that report, we wouldn't be fighting with the data platform like we are now. If we go back and look at that published data, we can clearly see that we forecasted these difficulties.

Sam: Yes, that situation was not ideal, but you win some and you lose some. You can't make the perfect call all the time.

Omar: True, but maybe if we follow the prescribed path of gathering data and doing research this time around, we can avoid unnecessary self-inflicted wounds. I've already published our initial findings, and we're close to concluding our in-depth analysis. I believe that with a little more time to finalize our data exploration, we can avoid the pitfalls we encountered previously. Haruto is also supportive of us taking this extra step to ensure that we're making the most informed decision.

Sam: I do want to avoid any repeat of last time's fallout. But here is my big challenge. How much more time are you suggesting? I don't know if we can hold off Alison much longer.

Omar: Just a few more weeks should suffice. I know it might seem like a lot, but I can help you message this to Alison. We can use the pain of moving too quickly without data to decide on our data platform as an example of why this is time well spent. This will allow us to thoroughly vet all aspects and bring everything to the table, ensuring that we make a decision that's sustainable and beneficial long-term.

Sam: Do me a favor.... Write a quick email that we can send to Alison. Using our past pain to buy more time might be the right move.

Omar: I definitely support this approach. I'll make sure that the team keeps moving with their exploration and findings and I'll send you that note that we can use to inform Alison.

Sam: Thanks, Omar. Talk soon.

In this Instant Message (IM) exchange, Omar tactfully addresses the need for a comprehensive review of data before making a decision on the new platform adoption. By reminding Sam of the previous issues and highlighting the importance of a thorough evaluation process, Omar effectively encourages a more measured approach to decision-making before the impending reaction from Sam places them back in the same position they were last time. This conversation illustrates his strategic communication skills and his commitment to ensuring that decisions are data-driven to prevent undesirable outcomes.

Summing It Up

Dealing with a Raw Nerve manager, characterized by their impulsive and emotionally driven decision-making, poses unique challenges in the workplace. This archetype, while capable of swift decisions, often risks overlooking detailed analysis and long-term implications, which can lead to suboptimal outcomes and increased workplace stress. However, through strategic communication, careful planning, and the cultivation of supportive networks, employees can effectively navigate and mitigate the challenges posed by this managerial style.

1. **Anticipate the Cravings:** Like any good dieter, anticipating The Raw Nerve manager's challenging behavior can yield positive results and help you apply coping strategies. If you've noticed that your manager exhibits Raw Nerve archetype traits, listen closely to their verbal and written communication. Become

extremely sensitive to the warning signals as they talk more about pressure, not being able to "buy time," or "delay" any longer. These are all subtle cues that this archetype uses to justify and signal that they're about to make (or have already made) the decision to react rather than respond.

2. **Strategic Communication:** Engage in open and ongoing dialogue that emphasizes the importance of data-driven decisions. Use tactful reminders of past outcomes when quick decisions did not yield the desired results, as seen in Omar's approach to reminding Sam about the fallout from previous quick decisions.

3. **Documentation and Thorough Analysis:** Maintain meticulous records and continue with thorough analytical processes despite pressures to expedite decisions. This ensures that all decisions are well-informed and backed by empirical evidence, minimizing the risk of negative repercussions. Even if the decision has already been made and the reaction is irreversible, still proceed with the publication of the documentation and the analysis. This evidence will stand as a warning to "future generations" of how disaster could be avoided if the process is followed.

4. **Building Coalitions:** Develop relationships with key stakeholders within and outside your immediate team, such as peers, skip-level managers, and influential colleagues like Omar did with Terry. These relationships can form a support network that can collectively influence and moderate The Raw Nerve's instincts by emphasizing a collaborative approach to decision-making.

5. **Empowerment Through Delegation:** Advocate for empowerment in decision-making processes within your scope of work. This not only enhances team morale but also reduces the direct impact of hasty managerial decisions on your immediate team's productivity and job satisfaction. Note that despite the empowerment agreement, you'll have to vigorously listen for warning signs that The Raw Nerve manager is about to subvert and undermine that agreement.

6. **Escalation With Caution:** Understand when and how to escalate concerns carefully. Escalation should be a strategic move, backed by solid evidence and pursued only after internal strategies to address impulsive decisions have been exhausted. The goal is to ensure that escalation is seen as constructive and necessary for the well-being of the team and the organization. Avoid incrimination, complaints, and castigation, and instead focus on support for the data-driven process executing to conclusion.

By integrating these strategies, employees can foster a workplace environment that tempers the challenges of working with a Raw Nerve manager. The ultimate goal is to transform potential vulnerabilities into strengths by encouraging more thoughtful, data-driven approaches to decision-making. This not only benefits the immediate team but also contributes positively to the broader organizational culture and success.

CHAPTER 8

The Attack Sub

Background

Zara's morning tranquility was abruptly shattered as her phone erupted with a barrage of urgent instant messages. Bleary-eyed and barely awake, she reached for the device, her heart rate accelerating with each notification. It was Elena, her boss, unleashing a torrent of directives that commanded her immediate attention. Overnight, Elena had been burdened with the formidable task of orchestrating an all-encompassing executive briefing on the latest data platform adoption statistics across the organization. The briefing, which was to encompass a detailed history of platform adoption, explain its selection process, and elaborate on metrics and OKRs regarding adoption costs and Return on Investment (ROI), was due by Thursday evening for a critical board presentation.

For Zara, the timing couldn't have been worse. Her week had been meticulously planned with team-building exercises and the final orchestration of significant programs set to conclude. What was supposed to be a carefully structured week was now under siege, her schedule blown apart by Elena's sudden demands.

Understanding the gravity of the task, Zara fired back a series of follow-up questions to Elena: How far back should the history go? What specific OKRs are crucial for the executive panel? Who exactly are we presenting to, and whose buy-in is critical? What's the main objective of this exercise, and what does the audience want to hear? What potential questions should the presentation preemptively address?

However, after setting the digital battleground with her initial salvo of messages, Elena submerged back into the depths of her responsibilities, becoming inexplicably silent. Her responses were crucial for navigating the murky waters ahead, yet she became unreachable.

Emails, instant messages, and even direct calls went unanswered. Zoom meetings that she attended offered no opportunity for discussion as she had to leave abruptly or remained muted throughout the sessions.

When Thursday arrived, Zara, having been forced to rely on assumptions and her best guesswork, presented the briefing slides. Despite her efforts to hit the mark, it was clear from Elena's abrupt interjection that the presentation had missed critical points. She voiced her frustration openly, criticizing the lack of alignment with the board's expectations and promising to work closely with Zara to refine the presentation. Yet, as days passed, Elena's promised guidance proved as elusive as her availability, plunging Zara once again into a state of professional limbo, having to guess at corrections with the same scant information as before.

This sequence of events is emblematic of The Attack Sub manager archetype. These are managers who run silent for extended periods of time, as if they dove under water and are unreachable. Suddenly, without prior warning or engagement, they violently surface unexpectedly with explosive and voluminous feedback or new directives that are not always calibrated well to producing good work products. This management style can often leave teams reeling from sudden shifts in focus and priorities, struggling to align with the leader's unspoken expectations and drowning in ambiguity and uncertainty as they try to assemble their best guess as to what the manager wanted.

The Archetype Defined

In the vast ocean of organizational management, The Attack Sub manager is a formidable and elusive figure. Like the stealthy vessels patrolling the unseen depths, these managers navigate the complexities of their roles beneath the surface, often out of sight and out of mind to their teams. They run deep and silent, conserving their visibility until the moment demands a sudden and decisive emergence. When they do surface, it's with a barrage of directives, evaluations assignments, and requirements—a salvo that can catch even the most prepared team off guard. Here are some key characteristics that commonly present in an Attack Sub manager.

Characteristics:

- **Stealth Operation:** The Attack Sub manager is rarely visible in daily operations, preferring to work in isolation. Communication is sporadic, and their presence is often felt more by the weight of their authority than by direct interactions.
- **Sudden Emergences:** Without warning, this manager will surface, often at critical junctures, delivering a flood of information, decisions, or changes in directives. This pattern of unexpected appearances and demands can disrupt ongoing workflows and throw planned strategies into chaos.
- **Minimal Feedback:** Between their appearances, there is little to no feedback or guidance. Teams are left to navigate the wake of their directives without much support, making it challenging to align ongoing work with managerial expectations.
- **Impact on Team Dynamics:** The unpredictable nature of The Attack Sub manager can lead to a tense and anxious workplace. Teams may struggle with uncertainty, not knowing when the next set of orders will come or what new priorities will be thrust upon them. This can stifle initiative and creativity, as team members may hesitate to make decisions independently for fear of conflicting with undeclared future directives.

The behavior of The Attack Sub manager archetype is largely driven by an interrupt-driven management style, often stemming from their challenges in handling the demands of a densely packed schedule. These managers are typically in high demand across the organization, leading to days filled with back-to-back meetings and an overwhelming influx of communications, including hundreds of unread emails and instant messages. This constant bombardment leaves little time for them to methodically work through their backlog or engage in proactive guidance. These managers are exceptionally talented and often experienced individuals who are simply in high demand as it relates to their presence in meetings, the volume of their email and other messages, and those vying for their attention and input. However, this overload can have a detrimental impact on organizational agility, innovation, and individual well-being as well as that of their teams.[*]

As a result, they are compelled to focus predominantly on immediate crises and looming deadlines—the "fires" that need urgent attention. This focus on crisis management necessitates a mode of operation where they surface sporadically, delivering rapid-fire directives to address pressing issues before quickly submerging back into the depths of their other responsibilities. This pattern is not merely a preference but a survival tactic in the high-stakes environment in which they operate, driven by the necessity to manage an overwhelming array of tasks and decisions. Consequently, their engagement with the team is episodic, marked by intense bursts of activity to tackle imminent disasters, followed by periods of minimal contact, during which time they are submerged in addressing other critical demands of their role. This leads to a dynamic where follow-up and sustained guidance are often sacrificed, fueling the cyclical nature of The Attack Sub's abrupt appearances and disappearances.

For employees under the command of an Attack Sub manager, the work environment can feel like navigating a minefield. Each day might pass without incident, yet the looming threat of a sudden managerial emergence keeps tension high. When the manager surfaces, the onslaught of tasks can be overwhelming, leaving little time for comprehension or adjustment. After delivering their orders, they disappear again, leaving their team to manage the fallout. This can foster a reactive, rather than proactive, workplace culture, where the focus shifts from strategic planning to short-term survival.

The impact on the team is profound. Morale can suffer under the weight of unpredictability and the constant pressure to quickly pivot without sufficient preparation or context. Collaboration may falter as team members, caught in a cycle of reaction rather than action, find it hard to synchronize their efforts without a consistent guiding presence.

---

[*] Deloitte Consulting LLP, n.d., "Fixing the Overload Problem at Work." Deloitte Insights, Accessed May 21, 2024.

For those who identify with working under an Attack Sub manager, recognizing this archetype is the first step in developing coping strategies that can help mitigate these challenges. Understanding the dynamics at play allows teams to better prepare for sudden directives, maintain a degree of operational readiness, and perhaps most importantly, support each other through the unpredictable ebbs and flows dictated by such a leadership style.

Coping Strategies

Coping with The Attack Sub manager archetype requires a blend of tactical and strategic approaches, designed to effectively navigate their sporadic engagement style and ensure that essential communication and guidance are maintained. Here are several coping strategies tailored to manage the dynamics posed by this challenging managerial style.

Channel Switching

Channel switching is a tactical, highly short-term strategy designed to capture the attention of an Attack Sub manager when a rapid response is crucial. The effectiveness of this strategy hinges on its sporadic use; overuse can lead to diminished returns as the novelty, which initially captures the manager's attention, wears off. The essence of channel switching lies in moving from one form of communication to another —such as transitioning from email to text or from text to a messaging app like Slack. This shift often breaks the pattern of everyday communication noise, momentarily drawing the manager's focus to the new channel.

This approach is particularly effective when timing is considered. For instance, reaching out early in the morning might catch the manager at a moment when they can afford a few cycles of focus, making them more likely to engage with the message. However, the content of these communications must be carefully managed; messages should be concise and focused on short, tactical items. If the message is too lengthy or laden with heavy stakes, requiring extensive context or significant decision-making, there is an elevated risk that the manager will quickly disengage and submerge again, rendering the channel switching ineffective. Therefore, this strategy should be reserved for situations where an immediate but brief interaction is essential to advancing day-to-day operations.

- **Implementation:** When you notice a lapse in response on one communication channel, such as email, promptly switch to a more immediate channel such as texting or instant messaging. This can help in capturing the manager's attention in the moment. Keep messages concise and focused on urgent matters to maximize the likelihood of a response.

- **Consideration:** Be prepared for quick shifts between communication channels as the manager's responsiveness may vary. It's essential to prioritize the urgency and relevance of your messages to avoid overloading any single channel. Also note that channel switching typically can't be used frequently, because essentially, you'll be bombarding the manager on multiple channels, thereby casting yourself fully into being ignored on all the channels. The driving factor behind why this coping strategy works is due to communication novelty in an unexpected channel. Frequency of use will mitigate the novelty, thereby rendering channel switching ineffective.

Putting It Into Practice

As Zara prepares for a crucial executive presentation dependent on finalizing a contract with a new technology partner, she faces the challenge of securing final approval from Elena, her manager, known for her Attack Sub archetype behavior. Aware of her pattern of minimal engagement followed by sudden, critical interventions, Zara strategically employs both email and text messaging to ensure timely communication and secure the necessary sign-off.

Subject: Final Approval Needed on Technology Partner Selection

Hi Elena,

Hope you're doing well. As we approach the culmination of our multiweek project to select a new technology partner, I wanted to ensure that all elements are aligned for a successful conclusion. We are at a critical juncture where the final budgeting exercise requires your review and approval before we can proceed to contract signing.

Attached you will find a detailed breakdown of the proposed budget along with the benefits this partnership is expected to bring to our organization. Your approval is crucial for moving forward, as it will allow us to send the contract to procurement for execution. Please review the attached document and let me know if there are any adjustments you'd like to make.

Looking forward to your input to finalize this important initiative. Please let me know by EOD Thursday if there are any concerns or changes needed.

Best regards,

Zara

This email has all the hallmarks of a concise communication email to an Attack Sub manager. It has

- Clear description of the requirement and need with context;
- A clear articulation of what involvement or action is needed;
- A time frame for action.

However, as Zara is familiar, these pressures result in significant challenges for employees of The Attack Sub manager archetype. She knows this email, even if it is read, will not result in the desired behavior of a response as called for in her message. As a result, she knows he's got to do something different to disrupt Elena's input filters while she's submerged so she can at least understand a task has landed for her, which requires immediate action. Zara, realizing all of this, utilizes channel switching to get the desired disruption and ostensibly her attention.

Follow-Up Text Message From Zara to Elena (Two Days Later)

Hi Elena, I sent you an email regarding the final approval needed for the technology partner budget. Could you please check it at your earliest convenience? We need your go-ahead to move forward by Thursday. Thanks!

Response From Elena to Zara's Text (One Minute Later)

Hi Zara, just saw your text. I'll review the documents and get back to you by noon today.

> In this scenario, Zara uses a strategic approach by first sending a detailed email to Elena outlining the necessary steps for final approval. Aware of Elena's Attack Sub archetype behavior, which includes surfacing unpredictably and often at the last minute, Zara ensures that she provides all necessary information in a concise and clear manner, documenting her communication for future reference. She then employs channel switching, a tactical move designed to capture Elena's attention more effectively. By following up with a text—a channel she rarely uses but expects will prompt a quicker response—Zara successfully receives the acknowledgment needed to proceed. This method not only secures the needed approval from Elena but also mitigates the risk of her surfacing unexpectedly with changes (or inaction in her accountable responsibilities) at the last minute, ensuring the project's smooth continuation toward its final stages.

Leverage the Power of Silent Agreement

Working with an Attack Sub manager can often feel like navigating a minefield, especially when their sporadic involvement leads to abrupt interferences that can undermine months of carefully planned projects and initiatives. To preemptively cope with this managerial style, one effective tactic is the use of proactive communication framed around the concept of silent agreement.

This approach involves sending a clear and concise email to the manager outlining your planned course of action for a particular project or task. The key is to provide a complete but succinct summary of the actions you intend to take and the rationale behind them, ensuring that all critical information is communicated upfront. At the end of this communication, it is crucial to include a line such as, "As described above, these are my plans and how I'm moving forward. Let me know if you think I should alter my plans to any degree. Otherwise, we'll be moving ahead as described above, next week."

Leveraging Silent Agreement: By closing your update with a statement like the one before, you are effectively going on record and requesting their input while also moving forward with your initiatives. If the manager does not respond, their silence can be interpreted as tacit approval of your actions. This tactic leverages the power of silent agreement, providing you with a form of documented consent that can be invaluable when the manager chooses to unexpectedly resurface and challenge the decisions made in their absence.

Mitigating Potential Damage: When an Attack Sub manager surfaces and attempts to disrupt the project's trajectory with new directives or feedback that is now too late, having this prior communication in hand can significantly reduce the impact. You can refer back to the email sent, highlighting their lack of response as a nod of approval to proceed as planned. This can help mitigate the potential damage by reminding them of the implicit consent they provided, making it harder for them to refute the decisions you've made based on their initial nonresponse.

Additional Considerations: There are some additional considerations associated with this plan, which include making sure you're not being sneaky and preying upon the fact that you know they won't read your emails. Sending a channel switching notification and documenting when you told them can lead you to help inform them prior to their big surfacing event and hopefully elicit feedback while they're submerged.

Channel Switching: If a quick response is required or if the manager typically does not engage deeply with emails, follow up through a different communication channel, like a brief text or instant message. This can ensure that your email has been noticed, yet still holds the manager accountable for the lack of response. It also allows you to be professionally above board, making sure you're not trying to be surreptitious and burying silent agreement stipulations in email where they aren't likely to read.

Documentation: Even though The Attack Sub manager doesn't engage through email or other electronic communication, it doesn't mean that they should not be held accountable. Reading electronic communication and responding is a minimal expectation that mostly all professionals have. Bearing this in mind, keep a well-organized record of all communications with the manager, especially those involving critical decisions and plans. This documentation will be crucial if discrepancies arise or if the manager's memory of events does not align with the actions taken.

By implementing this strategy, you can create a safeguard against the disruptive tendencies of an Attack Sub manager, protecting the integrity of your projects and maintaining continuity in your strategic direction, even in the face of managerial unpredictability. Note that this is considered a tactical strategy to deal with blast radius minimization when The Attack Sub manager does surface to upend your plans.

Putting It Into Practice

As Zara prepares for a critical phase in a transformational project, she faces the challenge of ensuring alignment with Elena, her manager known for her Attack Sub archetype behavior, which includes sporadic involvement and abrupt decision-making interferences. To proactively manage potential disruptions and secure approval for crucial project decisions, Zara crafts a strategic email to Elena, aiming to leverage the power of silent agreement.

Subject: Budget Allocation and Engineering Consultant Plan for Transformational Project

Hi Elena,

I hope this message finds you well. I am writing to outline the budget allocation and operational plan for the upcoming two-month execution phase of our transformational project. Given the scope and impact of this initiative, I intend to allocate a significant portion of our budget to bringing in specialized consulting engineers who will assist in building and optimizing the platform. This strategic decision is designed to enhance our technical capacity swiftly and ensure that we meet our project milestones with the highest standards of quality.

The rationale for involving external expertise stems from our need to integrate advanced technologies that exceed our current internal capabilities. This approach not only accelerates our development timeline but also mitigates risks associated with project complexities. As described before, these are my plans and how I'm moving forward. Please let me know if you think I should alter my plans to any degree.

Thank you for your attention to this matter. **I look forward to your input and will proceed with the outlined steps unless advised otherwise by Friday.**

Best regards,
Zara

This email from Zara to Elena effectively uses the strategy of silent agreement by clearly outlining the planned course of action and asking for any objections or modifications with a time box surrounding it. This is the silent approval as outlined in bold previously. She clearly articulates how she's going to proceed unless she hears from her (which more than likely she knows she won't). This documentation will serve as an insurance policy of sorts so if and when Elena surfaces and takes issue with her budget allocation, she can apprise her that she's already informed her and given her a chance to weigh-in prior to her execution. Furthermore, Zara should employ channel switching, and perhaps text Elena to let her know that she's sent this message so she's not surreptitiously hiding a silent approval from her deliberately. This approach provides Elena with the opportunity to voice any concerns while allowing Zara to move forward with the plans unless she hears otherwise, thereby securing tacit approval through her nonresponse.

Hold Team Offsites

The Team Offsite technique is a proactive approach designed to manage and mitigate the disruptive tendencies of Attack Sub managers. By removing the manager from the usual business environment for an extended period, the team can refocus and reconnect the manager with the core work, mission, and strategic priorities of the team. This setting provides neutral ground where employees can openly discuss how the manager's sporadic appearances and decision-making impact team morale, often causing anxiety and uncertainty.

An Emotionally Intelligent Intervention: During the offsite, the team has the opportunity to engage in candid conversations about the consequences of The Attack Sub behavior, including the stress and complications it introduces into ongoing projects. These discussions aim to foster a deeper understanding in the manager of the effects their style has on team dynamics and productivity. Furthermore, the offsite allows for the development of key communication agreements, such as a service level agreement (SLA) for responsiveness, particularly when crucial decisions are needed. This agreement acknowledges the manager's heavy workload while establishing a mutual expectation for timely communication, ensuring that both the manager's and the team's needs are met.

Held With Regularity to Reground the Attack Sub: To maintain effectiveness, the team offsite should be a recurring event. Regular sessions help recalibrate and realign the manager and team, especially when Attack Sub behaviors reemerge. These offsites serve not only as a checkpoint for reviewing progress and adjusting strategies but also as a vital mechanism for sustaining open lines of communication and reinforcing the collaborative agreements established during previous meetings. By continuously engaging in these strategic retreats, teams can create a more stable and predictable working environment, even in the presence of an Attack Sub managerial style.

Putting It Into Practice

Zara: (*Walking by Elena's office and popping her head in*) "Hey Elena, got a minute?"

Elena: "Of course, Zara. What's up?"

Zara: "I just wanted to express how much I appreciate you agreeing to join us for the upcoming offsite. It really means a lot to the team, and I think it's going to be incredibly valuable for all of us."

Elena: "I'm glad to hear that. I'm looking forward to stepping away from the daily grind and focusing on the team for a bit. I feel like it's been forever since I was able to have enough time to spend with them."

Zara: "Absolutely, and your presence there will really signal your confidence and trust in the team. It's a fantastic opportunity to not just touch base but really engage deeply with everyone's ideas and concerns in a way that daily operations just don't allow."

Elena: "I can see how that would be beneficial. What do you have planned for us?"

Zara: "Well, part of the offsite will be dedicated to discussing our workflows and the impacts of decisions—kind of a state-of-the-union from the team's perspective. There's been some feedback about how the sporadic nature of your time slicing across your scope of responsibilities can tend to disrupt project flow and causes a bit of anxiety."

Elena: "I am underwater almost all the time, so I get that. It's important for me to understand that better. How do you think we should address it?"

Zara: "I think creating a safe space for honest feedback will be crucial. We'll facilitate sessions where team members can share their experiences and suggest improvements without fear of negative repercussions. It's not about pointing fingers but rather about finding ways to enhance our collaboration."

Elena: "That sounds like a good approach. I want to make sure we're all moving forward together, and if there are adjustments I need to make, I'm open to hearing about them."

Zara: "That's great to hear, Elena. And honestly, your infectious optimism and leadership can really help reinvigorate the team. This offsite could also be a springboard for us to establish some new behavioral norms that focus on boosting morale, productivity, and the way we handle feedback."

Elena: "I'm ready to do whatever it takes, Zara. Let's make sure we come out of this with some strong action points and a clearer path forward."

Zara: "Perfect, Elena. Thanks again for being so open to this. I'll make sure the agenda reflects our goals and maximizes our time together. Looking forward to it!"

Elena: "Me too, Zara. See you there."

In this dialogue, Zara uses emotionally intelligent communication techniques to prepare Elena for the offsite, highlighting its benefits and the positive impact her active participation could have on the team. She tactfully introduces the issues caused by her sporadic engagement without being confrontational, framing the offsite as a constructive opportunity for everyone to realign and strengthen their collaborative efforts. She uses affirming statements wrapped in gratitude to not only thank her but also provide her positive reinforcement that she's making the right choice to spend her time focused on this activity.

Summing It Up

In the vast ocean of organizational management, The Attack Sub archetype represents a challenging yet not uncommon style of leadership. This archetype, likened to a submarine that operates hidden beneath the surface, emerges unexpectedly to unleash feedback, directives and decisions before disappearing again. This sporadic involvement leads to sudden and often disruptive impacts on projects and initiatives, which can destabilize teams and derail carefully laid plans.

The Attack Sub manager's unpredictable appearances and interventions can significantly disrupt team dynamics, lowering morale and affecting the quality of work. Teams may struggle with constant uncertainty, unsure when the next directive will torpedo their current efforts. This can lead to a reactive rather than proactive work environment, where long-term strategies are sacrificed for short-term damage control. The suddenness of decision-making can also lead to errors and oversight, as there isn't sufficient time to weigh all options or consider the broader implications. For strategic or material organizational initiatives, this will have a damaging lasting impact, delaying implementation timelines and demolishing progress.

1. **Tactical Communication Techniques:** Utilizing techniques like channel switching to maintain communication and preemptive emails that seek silent agreement can help mitigate the blast radius while The Attack Sub manager is submerged. These methods ensure that there's a record of interaction and implied consent, which can be referenced when the manager surfaces.

2. **Damage Control:** When The Attack Sub surfaces, having a plan in place to mitigate the impact of their decisions is crucial. This includes having fallback plans, maintaining flexible project scopes, and ensuring that all team members are prepared to adapt quickly. This also includes having a spate of documentation where "silent approval" was obtained to prove they were informed.

3. **Anticipation and Engagement:** Like dealing with many complex managerial archetypes, successful navigation around an Attack Sub manager relies heavily on anticipation. Recognizing the patterns of their appearances and understanding their triggers can help in preparing for their impact. Coping strategies for this archetype vary from tactical maneuvers to more comprehensive damage control methods.

4. **Strategic Offsites:** Perhaps one of the most effective strategies is engaging the manager in periodic strategic offsites. These sessions pull the manager out of the business's day-to-day operations and provide an opportunity for deep reconnection with the team. During these offsites, the team can candidly discuss the negative impacts of The Attack Sub behavior and work together

to establish more effective communication habits and responsive strategies. It also allows the manager to see firsthand the
consequences of their management style and fosters a better
understanding of the need for change.

By employing these strategies, teams can create a more stable
environment that accommodates the unique challenges of working with
an Attack Sub manager. These efforts not only protect the integrity of
projects but also improve team morale, ensuring that the organization
can navigate successfully through the unpredictable waters of management.

CHAPTER 9

The LIFO (Last In, First Out)

Background

Luke had been meticulously preparing for weeks, orchestrating a monumental project kickoff that promised to redefine the organization's approach to AI. His efforts had not been minor. He spent days aligning departments, divisions, and business lines from across the globe all to create a harmonized push toward innovation. The goal was to convene in New York for an envisioning summit, a strategic initiative that would catalyze the integration of AI across all sectors of the organization. The day had finally come, and the large, cavernous conference room buzzed with anticipation, hosting about 50 key personnel ranging from engineers and technology leaders to vice presidents of the business.

As Luke approached the podium, ready to harness the collective energy and intellect of the room to propel the organization into a new era, he was unexpectedly intercepted by Ana. Emerging from the wings of the conference stage and beckoning to Luke just as he was about to begin his keynote to kick off the weeklong event, he could tell she was brimming with urgent news. Her interruption was as abrupt as it was ill-timed. She relayed that a new initiative, passed down by Haruto just the previous night, was now taking precedence. As it turned out, Ana related that in her estimation, this new directive would require a massive reallocation of engineering and technology resources—resources that had already been committed to the AI project Luke was leading. Finally, the nail was driven into the coffin of the project, just seconds before Luke was about to kick it off as she relayed the brunt of the bad news. His initiative would be delayed until further notice while the organization retooled around this latest initiative.

Luke's frustration was palpable. Amid the confusion and the crowded room waiting for the summit to commence, he struggled to comprehend Ana's reasoning. Questions flooded his mind: Why hadn't Ana negotiated the importance of their well-planned AI initiative, which had already secured funding and resources? Why was her immediate reaction to redirect these resources instead of considering an expansion of the team or other avenues to accommodate the new project? Most importantly, why choose that critical moment to announce such a shift, potentially undermining the entire effort before it even began?

It was a pattern of behavior he'd seen before. Ana routinely focused on providing priority to the most recent initiative or project that leadership asked her for. She frequently shredded existing project resources, destroyed ongoing initiatives by cannibalizing their resources, snatching teams from completing work and assignments to swarm reflexively around the newest ask from management without any thought given to the impact such a reallocation would have on the organization. In the moments before Luke would have to address the audience about the catastrophic disruption, he realized that the last directive she received would always win. It was almost a reflexive behavior. As he turned to address the audience, struggling to figure out what to say, he realized that he needed to figure out not only the best way to rescue his initiative but how to manage upward, to help Ana grow so that she could consider a broader perspective. Otherwise, her team would end the year without any palpable results and the organization would suffer if they kept getting their major initiatives disrupted by Ana's behavior.

The Archetype Defined

This scenario epitomizes The LIFO (Last In, First Out) manager archetype, characterized by prioritizing the most recent directives at the expense of ongoing projects, regardless of their significance or investment. Ana's approach, typical of LIFO managers, reflects a reactive management style that focuses on immediate demands without a comprehensive evaluation of their impact on established plans. This management style can lead to significant strategic disarray, demoralizing teams and destabilizing projects that have been months in the making. For Luke and his team, Ana's last-minute pivot not only jeopardized the launch of a pivotal project but also signaled a broader issue of misalignment within the organization's leadership, challenging the coherence and efficacy of their strategic initiatives.

Managers exhibiting LIFO characteristics often struggle under the weight of overwhelming workloads and high demands from multiple directions. The continuous influx of urgent tasks compels them to prioritize whatever arrives last, thereby adopting a reactive rather than a proactive approach to management. This can be exacerbated by deficiencies in organizational and time management skills, where managers might lack the ability to effectively prioritize tasks based on their importance or deadlines. Consequently, these managers often handle tasks in opposite of the sequence they are received, which appears to be a straightforward strategy but often leads to neglect of longer-term projects.

Furthermore, decision fatigue can play a significant role in LIFO behavior, where the quality of decisions deteriorates after making numerous decisions in a row. Managers may default to focusing only on new information or tasks that seem urgent, neglecting projects that do not demand immediate attention but are crucial in the long run. Additionally, a fear of confrontation or conflict might prevent these managers from negotiating realistic expectations with senior leadership, leading them to accept new assignments without the necessary resources or adjustments in timelines (note this is similar to The Order Taker management archetype). This is often compounded by a lack of strategic vision, which makes it difficult for them to assess the long-term implications of their decisions on the organization's broader objectives.

The organizational environment also significantly influences LIFO tendencies. If the culture or reward system within a company emphasizes quick responses to new challenges, managers are likely to continue adopting a LIFO approach, as it is reinforced by positive feedback or incentives. Additionally, the nature of the way we work in the digital age adds another layer of complexity with a constant barrage of emails and notifications, making recent issues seem more pressing due to their visibility. Here are some ways to spot a LIFO manager.

Characteristics:

- **Reactive Rather Than Proactive:** LIFO managers often respond to the latest input or demand, sidelining earlier commitments and projects. This approach typically results in a pattern where new tasks are continuously placed at the top of their priority list, pushing older yet critical initiatives further down or off the slate entirely. Note that usually teams are still accountable for these older initiatives, making the team's life extremely difficult.

- **Destructive Impact on Team Morale and Productivity:** The unpredictability and inconsistency of LIFO management can significantly impact team morale. Team members may feel that their efforts are wasted when projects are abruptly deprioritized or discarded, leading to frustration and decreased productivity. It also adds significant stress as deprioritization by The LIFO manager doesn't mean the team is free from accountability of those items.

- **Short-Term Focus:** These managers are often so absorbed by immediate pressures that they lose sight of long-term goals and strategies. This short-sightedness can hinder the organization's ability to plan and execute strategically, affecting overall growth and adaptation to market changes.

For those working for a LIFO manager archetype, it's imperative to understand their motivations, the challenges that they face daily and to determine the best way to help them manage. Ultimately, we want to encourage The LIFO manager archetype to avert their instinctual behavior when a new demand arises from leadership by getting them to take a breath, pause, and ask themselves, "I know I could pull the trigger, reallocate resources, and swarm on this new request, but what would that do to all of the projects and outcomes my teams are working on for the organization?" Achieving this level of instinct suspension, awareness, and thinking can take a significant amount of managing upwards from employees.

Coping Strategies

To effectively manage a LIFO manager, employees must adopt specific strategies that anticipate and mitigate the challenges posed by this management style. LIFO managers, characterized by their tendency to prioritize the most recent tasks or projects over ongoing ones, can disrupt planned activities and create a chaotic work environment. Employees need to ensure constant communication, strategically reminding the manager of ongoing projects' importance and deadlines to keep them on the radar. It's also beneficial to document all interactions and agreed-upon priorities to hold the manager accountable and provide a reference when priorities are suddenly shifted. Setting clear expectations and using tactful reminders can help align the manager's focus with the team's long-term goals, thereby maintaining project continuity and minimizing the disruptive impact of their last-minute changes. These proactive steps form the foundation for a more detailed discussion on coping strategies that can help teams navigate the unpredictability of working with a LIFO manager, ensuring that critical projects are not sidelined by new distractions.

Managing a LIFO manager involves tactical and strategic actions to minimize disruption and instill a more balanced approach to project prioritization. Here are some coping strategies that you can use to tackle working with this manager archetype.

Tackle Immediate Disruptions Through Gentle Questioning

When a LIFO manager abruptly shifts priorities, causing potential harm to ongoing projects, it's crucial to react constructively. While it may be galling, frustrating, and maddening all at the same time, especially if it's a repeated behavior, take the time to process these emotions before reengaging with your LIFO manager. Once you've given yourself space to react, focus on managing upward through empathy and understanding (something that's hard to do when you're seeing red). When ready, begin by fully understanding the new request—ask pointed questions to clarify its urgency and importance. Questions such as the following:

"Have you considered how this new directive impacts our current commitments?"

"Do the stakeholders understand the consequences of diverting resources from our existing projects?"

Gentle Questioning Highlighting Consequences: These questions can prompt the manager to think more critically about the implications of their decisions and instinctive commitment. Utilize this moment to clearly outline the potential negative impacts of hastily changing directions, not only on the organization's operational flow but also on team morale. Present well-structured data and forecasts that illustrate these consequences, ensuring that your arguments are grounded in tangible outcomes. The source of these structured forecasts can be generated from cost projections, resource models, and milestones from existing projects that are already executing and are prime to suffer disastrous consequences if an unplanned shift occurs.

Triage and Proposal to Leadership: Accompany your analysis with a thoughtful recommendation that leverages a structured triage process (or refers to an existing process if you already have one established). This process will help assess and prioritize tasks based on their urgency and importance, providing a clear framework for integrating new tasks without disrupting ongoing projects. Note that this is remarkably similar to coping with The Order Taker management archetype. Suggest collaboratively crafting a proposal to present to leadership, one that not only respects the urgency of the new initiative but also advocates for a phased and realistic integration into the current workload. Volunteering to do the "heavy lifting" in this presentation is favorable to a busy LIFO manager who won't have time to consider owning it themselves.

Document and Share With Peer Groups: While your recommendation might not be immediately embraced (if ever), document your proposal formally after discussing it with your manager and share this documentation with relevant stakeholders and peer groups (with their full knowledge ahead of time). By doing this, you ensure broader visibility of your proactive and strategic approach, showcasing your commitment to the organization's long-term success and stability. This visibility not only strengthens your position but also encourages a more informed and collective approach to managing changes, potentially swaying the decision-making process toward a more balanced outcome.

Much like the Order Taker archetype, harmonious compliance is usually behind The LIFO's behavior. By working with The LIFO manager to generate a balanced message of "Can versus Should" plus a recommendation, employees can satisfy the need of the manager for harmony, while providing a platform to manage strategic projects and programs without significant disruption.

Putting It Into Practice

Luke and the other vice presidents connect to the Zoom meeting on time, but as usual, Ana connects five minutes late, her expression tense with urgency. Without preamble or meeting small talk, she drops a bombshell that had already torpedoed Luke's offsite earlier.

> **Ana:** "I just came from a meeting with Haruto and Alison. They're pushing for a massive pivot—focusing entirely on stabilizing our application platform across the organization. This is now our top priority, which means significant resource reallocation from both support and engineering as well as your team Luke as I told you earlier."
>
> The room falls silent, the weight of her words sinking in. Luke feels a familiar dread; this shift could effectively dismantle the momentum of his AI project as well as jeopardize several key initiatives his peers are working on. Swallowing the resurgence of disbelief and anger, he draws upon an inner calm and a desire to help Ana and the rest of his team make progress. After a moment to gather his thoughts, Luke addresses Ana, employing his well-practiced

coping strategy to deal with the fallout by tackling this latest disruption head on through key questions.

Luke: "Ana, I have a suggestion if you're open to it. I think we all know we want to comply with Haruto and Alison's needs. I'm thinking that we can certainly help plot a course that allows us to do that in the fullness of time. This way, we might be able to find a way to meet the new need without torpedoing existing valuable and funded work. I know that the teams would love to finish what they've already started and are currently accountable for. Wouldn't it be great for you and for all of us to get some wins under our belt before sacrificing progress to strike out on a new adventure?"

Ana: "Of course Luke, but we have to be good at pivoting. We can't dig our heels in here. Wins are great but showing that we're pulling in the same direction is equally important."

Luke takes in Ana's rebuttal, practicing active listening and summarizing her concerns while making a recommendation at the same time to conduct a data-driven proposal of the impact of pivoting and a more holistic and strategic path forward.

Luke: "I definitely get the need for our team to demonstrate that we're in the same boat. Any response that appears to make us look like we're saying 'no' would not go over well for all the reasons you mentioned. I'm recommending something a bit different than just saying 'we can't do that.' Before we proceed, shouldn't we discuss how this shift aligns with our ongoing projects? For instance, let's spend some time considering the long-term impacts this shift could have, especially on the AI initiative, which has substantial backing and expected ROI. Once we have that, we can then figure out a way to potentially pivot to address the new initiative without blowing up existing work, reorganizing teams and yanking people from projects that they're just about to complete. This way, we can still hit our goals, complete valuable work to the organization and be seen as responding to the pivot."

Ana pauses, her brow furrowing.

Ana: "That sounds like having our cake and eating it too. I'm suspicious of any solution that promises everything…. Haruto and Alison were quite adamant, and it seemed urgent."

Luke nods, understanding the pressure but also recognizing a gap in strategic handling.

Luke: "I appreciate the urgency, Ana, but what if we took a comprehensive approach? What if I put together an impact analysis just for our team? It could outline how we might balance this new directive with our current commitments. This way, we can present a plan to leadership that shows we're responsive yet strategic. Together, we can all see if there are ways to fold in this new initiative to existing work, delay the new initiative to start after a project completes, or recommend hiring new resources to address the new effort."

Seeing an opportunity, Luke continued.

Luke: "Also, if we got organizational support for our proposal, it wouldn't just be us informing leadership. It would be those division heads and executive vice presidents whose work would suffer if we just randomly abandoned existing projects in favor of a new initiative. I think it's crucial that we involve all division heads in this analysis. If we can unify our approach, it might give us a stronger position to propose a more feasible timeline and resource allocation that won't compromise our existing strategic projects."

Ana, resistance to the idea began to erode at the suggestion, signaled wordlessly to Luke that on some level she'd heard what sounded like an equitable plan. Luke knew, however, that she wasn't completely sold, but he took her acquiescence as a good sign of progress.

Ana: "Don't spend too much time on the analysis. I don't want you to waste a lot of cycles figuring this out. Share it once you have it with the team and then we can figure out what this simultaneous response looks like. Let's make sure we're all on the same page and bring something concrete back to Haruto and Alison."

In this conversation, Luke utilized a combination of emotional intelligence and empathy to understand Ana's true motives and perspectives. When he disagreed with her, he negotiated though the disagreement by appealing to what Ana's scope of responsibilities were (to have her team execute and accrue positive wins). He also folded in her focus on urgency, but painted a picture where all stakeholders could unite and define an outcome where they aren't saying "no" to leadership, but also not abandoning work. Luke's proposal not only aims to mitigate the disruptive impact of the sudden shift but also leverages collective leadership to ensure strategic continuity. By involving the division heads, he fosters a unified front, turning a challenging situation into an opportunity for collaborative problem-solving.

Prioritize and Triage

Navigating the challenges of working under a LIFO manager can feel overwhelming, but there is a beacon of hope in implementing structured and strategic practices that bring clarity and order to the chaos. By embracing thorough documentation and a robust triage and prioritization system, you create a foundation that can significantly influence your manager's decision-making process for the better.

Start by diligently maintaining detailed records of all projects, including their statuses, timelines, and allocated resources. This isn't just about keeping track; it's about crafting a clear narrative of each project's journey and its value to the organization. When a new project surfaces, carefully assess and document how its demands might impact the existing workload. This proactive approach not only prepares you for informed discussions but also arms you with evidence to support the continuity of crucial projects.

Further, establish a dynamic triage system that categorizes projects by their urgency and importance. This system isn't just a tool for organization—it's a strategic ally in your interactions with your manager. Regular reviews of a project backlog, conducted together with your manager, will keep both current and forthcoming projects in clear, prioritized view. This consistent visibility helps your LIFO manager appreciate the broader landscape of ongoing initiatives, encouraging a more balanced approach to new and existing tasks.

These practices are more than just administrative duties; they are your lifeline in steering your LIFO manager toward more thoughtful and impactful leadership. By implementing these strategies, you not only safeguard your team's efforts from being sidelined by the newest demand but also foster an environment where strategic priorities guide decision-making. This approach offers a hopeful pathway to transforming potential managerial pitfalls into opportunities for greater efficiency and success.

Putting It Into Practice

In a brightly lit conference room, Luke and Terry stand before a large whiteboard filled with Gantt charts, milestones, dates, and cost analyses. They are deeply engaged in quantifying the impacts of a sudden strategic shift directed by Ana that could derail Terry's projects. Terry has cleared his schedule to collaborate with Luke as he realized that many of his projects would be adversely affected if Ana elects to give in to her LIFO manager tendencies and shift resources and abandon projects.

Luke points to the chart, his marker hovering over the current timeline.

> **Luke:** "Terry, if we pivot completely to this new directive now, it's going to halt all progress not only on your projects but the other divisions as well. Let's quantify what that means in terms of opportunity cost and overall impact to the organization."
>
> Terry nods, looking thoughtfully at the figures.
>
> **Terry:** "Right, let's see the numbers. If you look just at my projects, they were projected to bring significant ROI by next quarter. These are real dollars that the organization is counting on. Halting them midway would mean a substantial financial setback and put us behind our competitors."
>
> Luke sketches out the financial implications, attaching dollar figures to delayed or potentially canceled outcomes.

Luke: "I had a feeling that was going to be the case when I convinced Ana to let us do this analysis. Based on our initial forecasts, stopping these projects could lead us to lose out on about $2 million in projected benefits over the next six months. There are two options I'm thinking of that get us around this problem."

With the numbers starkly presented, they proceed to brainstorm alternatives. Luke draws two new paths on the Gantt chart.

Luke: "Option one. We could delay the start of this new initiative until your first project is completed. It would mean a clean transition of resources and preserved ROI for the ongoing projects. The downside is we'd have to tell leadership they'll have to wait if we don't want to lose a competitive advantage and $2 million."

He then outlined a second approach.

Luke: "Option two involves a more gradual integration of the new directive. We start slowly, ramping up as resources roll off from finished projects. It spreads the load more evenly and mitigates sudden resource drains, but the downside is that it's not a full-fledged project kickoff for the new scope of work."

Terry, analyzing both options, feels a growing confidence.

Terry: "I believe this approach, especially the gradual integration, could resonate well with Alison and Haruto. It shows we're not just reacting hastily. Instead, we're ensuring that our response is thoughtful, data-driven, and structured to safeguard ongoing work while still aligning with the new strategic priorities. And we're giving them realistic options that they can choose between, as well as our recommendation."

Luke: "Exactly. We're demonstrating responsible stewardship of our resources and commitment to the organization's broader goals. Let's document these scenarios in detail and prepare a presentation that clearly lays out our proposed strategies along with the projected impacts and benefits. You and I can connect with Ana in the morning and get her support. With you there, I'm sure she'll see the wisdom in it."

As they finalize their session, both Luke and Terry feel prepared to advocate a well-reasoned proposal to convince Ana first and leadership second, together. Their collaborative effort not only strengthens their case but also highlights the strategic foresight in managing project transitions effectively. This proactive approach ensures that they are not merely reacting to new directives but are actively engaging in responsible and strategic planning that considers the full spectrum of organizational impact.

Educate Through Persistent Communication

Transforming the mindset of a LIFO manager can be achieved through persistent and educational communication. It's about engaging your manager regularly with insights that illuminate the value of balanced project management and strategic planning. Share compelling success stories and relevant data from both within and outside your organization that demonstrate the tangible benefits of a consistent and thoughtful approach. This isn't just about relaying information; it's about crafting a narrative that resonates with the manager, showing them how sustained focus on strategic goals, rather than knee-jerk reactions to the latest demands, can significantly enhance outcomes for the entire team and the organization at large.

By fostering an environment where strategic discussions are commonplace, you help your manager see beyond the immediacy of new tasks and appreciate the broader impact of their decisions. This continuous educational dialogue encourages a shift from reactive to proactive leadership, offering a beacon of hope for those struggling under the pressure of LIFO tendencies. It's a way to slowly but surely guide your manager toward a perspective where long-term success is the focal point, empowering them to lead with vision rather than impulse.

By implementing these strategies, employees can effectively manage the challenges posed by a LIFO manager and help them evolve into a more strategic and considerate leader. This approach not only safeguards ongoing projects but also enhances the manager's ability to contribute positively to the organization's long-term success.

Putting It Into Practice

In a spacious conference room, Ana's vice presidents, including Luke's team of project and program managers are gathered for a quarterly review. Judy, the program director, has just presented a comprehensive overview of the status of Ana's programs, detailing milestones, achievements, and forecasted resource utilization against the plan.

> **Judy:** "As we can see, our current resource allocation and project timelines are on track, with key dependencies between programs carefully managed to optimize our outputs and ROI."
>
> **Luke:** "Thanks, Judy, for that detailed update. Ana, I want to call to your attention, that this overview not only highlights the achievements of each program but also showcases the synergies between them. These connections have allowed us to accommodate a more gradual approach to the new initiative, which could have otherwise been quite disruptive to the achievements Judy just went through."

Luke continues, his tone earnest, addressing Ana directly.

> **Luke:** "This strategic overview is crucial, Ana. It shows when each program will deliver tangible ROI to the organization. More importantly, by triaging our efforts and collaborating closely with Terry and your other vice presidents, we developed two solid options for leadership. This approach ensured that we didn't sacrifice our revenue streams or competitive edge just because a new initiative fell into our laps."
>
> **Ana:** (*Listening intently, nods*) "I see your point, Luke. The data presented today does make a compelling argument for a balanced approach. I must admit, the gradual integration option seems to minimize risks significantly."
>
> **Luke:** "Exactly. Our goal was to ensure that any new directives could be integrated without overturning our current strategic commitments. Judy and I, along with our peers, are prepared to handle similar situations in the future by applying the same methodical analysis. We can quickly put together a set of options that protect our ongoing work while addressing any new priorities."

Ana: (*Pausing to consider*) "Alright, Luke. I appreciate the foresight and coordination you've shown here. Let's make this our standard playbook. Whenever a new priority emerges, I expect this level of analysis and collaborative planning. It's clear that this not only preserves our current investments but also prepares us better for unforeseen shifts."

Luke: "Thank you, Ana. You can count on us to maintain this standard. Judy and I, along with our teams, will ensure that our strategic objectives are always aligned with the organization's broader goals, even in the face of new challenges."

As the meeting wraps up, there is a sense of accomplished collaboration in the room. Ana's initial reluctance has turned into acknowledgment of the strategic value brought by Luke and his team's approach. This dialogue exemplifies how educating and communicating about the benefits of strategic project management can turn potential disruptions into opportunities for reinforcement of team capabilities and alignment with organizational goals.

Summing It Up

Navigating the challenges posed by a LIFO manager requires a strategic blend of understanding, anticipation, and proactive communication. LIFO managers, characterized by their tendency to prioritize new tasks over ongoing ones, can create significant disruptions within teams and projects. Understanding the motivations behind this behavior, such as overwhelming workloads, decision fatigue, and a lack of strategic vision, is crucial for developing effective coping strategies.

Tackle Immediate Disruptions With Questions: The first step in dealing with a disruptive torpedo from The LIFO manager is to process the shock, awe, and frustration as Luke did when his efforts on his project was literally destroyed before it began. After he was able to process his emotions, he pivoted to understanding The LIFO behavior and helping Ana by asking carefully crafted questions about the strategic impact of a reflexive decision. Utilize gentle questioning to help buy time to conduct an analysis, with your manager's peers and stakeholders, so that you can develop options that are backed by the whole team. Try to get your LIFO manager on board by reflecting the fact that you're not saying "no," but in fact, you're just identifying what "yes" means and what that would cost the organization. This is extremely useful when dealing with the fallout after a LIFO manager drops a disruptive pivot into the team.

Prioritize and Triage: Maintain meticulous records of all projects, highlighting how each aligns with the organization's long-term goals (utilizing a mature program management practice to help with this data). Use this data in discussions to help The LIFO manager see the bigger picture and understand the impacts of shifting priorities on previously established projects.

Collaborate with the manager to develop a system that evaluates projects based on urgency and importance. This structured approach can aid the manager in making more informed decisions about where to allocate resources and attention.

- When new directives emerge, work together to assess their impact and develop comprehensive proposals that consider the needs of all ongoing projects. Engage other stakeholders in this process to ensure that any plan of action has broad support and is aligned with the organization's overall objectives.

Proactive Communication and Education: Continually communicate the benefits of balanced project management. Share success stories and relevant data that emphasize how a consistent approach can lead to better outcomes for the team and the organization. This helps educate the manager about the value of strategic thinking over reactive decision-making. Implement scheduled sessions to review all active and upcoming projects. These meetings not only keep projects on the manager's radar but also provide a forum for discussing the strategic importance of each initiative, helping to stabilize priorities and prevent disruptive shifts.

- Utilize these strategies consistently to help LIFO managers become more deliberate and less disruptive in their decision-making. For example, as seen in the dialogue with Ana, Luke successfully used these methods to mitigate the impact of sudden strategic shifts. By preparing a detailed impact analysis and involving other key stakeholders, Luke demonstrated a proactive approach that not only safeguarded ongoing projects but also positioned the team as strategic thinkers capable of handling unexpected challenges.

Managing a LIFO manager effectively hinges on your ability to anticipate their needs, educate them on the consequences of their actions, and engage them in strategic planning. By implementing these coping strategies, you can help transform potentially chaotic management styles into opportunities for growth and development, ensuring that both the team's and the organization's goals are met.

PART 2

Coping Recommendations and Personal Growth

CHAPTER 10

Essential Coping Skills

In navigating the complexities of the modern workplace, certain coping skills emerge as essential for maintaining resilience, fostering growth, and ensuring success. These skills form a "professional substrate"—a foundational layer of good, common practices that can help professionals thrive despite the myriad of challenges they may encounter. Drawing from the previous recommendations, there are five key groupings of these coping skills: Anticipation and Proactive Planning, Emotional Intelligence and Empathy, Effective Communication, Self-Sufficiency and Independence, and Balancing Crisis with Stability. Each grouping, along with its subcomponents, offers a comprehensive approach to professional development and effective management.

Anticipation and Proactive Planning

Anticipation and proactive planning are fundamental to staying ahead in a dynamic work environment. By foreseeing potential challenges and preparing in advance, professionals can mitigate risks and turn obstacles into opportunities. Strategic thinking enhances this approach, ensuring that long-term goals are always in sight. The archetypes identified earlier, help you understand and identify challenging behaviors in your leaders that will help you grow to anticipate their idiosyncrasies. Anticipation is the best way to "prevent fires."

Anticipate Issues: Regularly anticipating potential challenges is a proactive strategy that can significantly reduce workplace stress and enhance productivity. By conducting regular check-ins, you can identify potential problems before they escalate. These check-in sessions function as probing exercises in which you can explore anticipated (or unanticipated) reactions or behavior and put in place strategies to deal with them, well before the audience widens (as well as the blast radius for harm). This foresight allows for timely interventions, such as mitigating negative manager behavior, reallocating resources or adjusting project timelines, thereby preventing crises and maintaining smooth operations. It also involves staying informed about industry trends and internal dynamics, which can help in predicting future challenges and preparing accordingly.

Strategic Thinking: Developing strategic thinking skills is crucial for long-term success. This involves looking beyond immediate tasks and considering the broader implications of decisions. Strategic thinkers align their actions with the organization's goals, ensuring that their efforts contribute to long-term growth and stability. They regularly assess their strategies to ensure that they remain relevant and effective in a changing environment. By prioritizing strategic thinking, professionals can create sustainable plans that drive continuous improvement and innovation.

To develop this skill, start by consistently setting aside time to reflect on your long-term objectives and how your current projects align with them. Engage in regular environmental scanning, which includes staying informed about industry trends, market dynamics, and organizational changes that could impact your work. Practice asking critical questions such as, "What are the potential long-term outcomes of this decision?" and "How does this align with our overarching goals?" Additionally, seek diverse perspectives by engaging with colleagues from different departments and levels within the organization, as this can provide valuable insights and foster innovative thinking. Embrace a mindset of continuous learning, actively seeking out new information, and being open to change and adaptation. By integrating these practices into your daily routine, you can enhance your ability to think strategically, making you better equipped to navigate complex challenges and drive sustainable success.

Emotional Intelligence and Empathy

Emotional intelligence and empathy are key to building strong, supportive relationships in the workplace. These skills enable professionals to navigate interpersonal dynamics effectively, fostering a positive and collaborative work environment. There is a key principle that will help you as you attempt to build empathy into your professional toolkit.

"People don't make logical decisions. They make emotional ones and seek logic and reason to support their choice."

Understanding that people often make emotional choices and then seek data to support their decisions is crucial for developing emotional intelligence and empathy. This insight highlights the importance of recognizing and addressing the emotional drivers behind people's actions. By acknowledging that emotions play a vital role in decision-making, professionals can approach interactions with greater empathy and sensitivity. This involves actively listening to colleagues and managers, validating their feelings, and responding in a way that acknowledges their emotional state or the reasons behind their choices. When communicating or negotiating, it's beneficial to connect on an emotional level first, establishing trust and rapport, before presenting logical arguments and data to support your points. This approach not only fosters a more supportive and collaborative work environment but also enhances your ability to influence and inspire others, ultimately leading to more effective and harmonious professional relationships.

> **Empathy and Positivity:** Showing empathy toward colleagues and managers is a powerful way to build trust and rapport. Empathy involves understanding and sharing the feelings of others, which can help in addressing concerns and resolving conflicts. By promoting positivity, professionals can create an inclusive and supportive atmosphere that encourages open communication and collaboration. This, in turn, enhances team cohesion and productivity, as individuals feel valued and understood.
>
> **Build Resilience and Support Networks:** Resilience is the ability to bounce back from setbacks, and it is crucial for maintaining mental and emotional well-being in the face of adversity.

Building resilience involves developing coping mechanisms, such as mindfulness and stress management techniques, which help maintain composure under pressure. Additionally, fostering strong support networks provides a safety net of resources and emotional support, which can be invaluable during challenging times. Colleagues, mentors, and professional groups can offer advice, encouragement, and practical assistance.

Foster Open Communication: Open and honest communication is the cornerstone of effective teamwork. By fostering an environment where individuals feel comfortable sharing their thoughts and feedback, professionals can ensure that issues are addressed promptly and transparently. This involves active listening, where one truly engages with the speaker and considers their perspective. Encouraging transparent feedback helps identify areas for improvement and fosters a culture of continuous learning and development. One clear way to begin this process is to heed the following statement.

"Always assume positive intent."

Another variation of this theme is even when there is negative intent, you should also heed the following.

"Quit Taking it Personally (QTIP)"

The QTIP principle, which stands for "Quit Taking It Personally," combined with always assuming positive intent, is vital in maintaining a healthy communication environment. By not taking feedback or comments personally, you can remain objective and open to constructive criticism. This mindset helps in managing your own emotional reactions and prevents defensive behaviors that can hinder effective communication. By assuming that feedback is meant to improve and not to harm, you can better focus on the content of the message rather than the delivery or perceived intent. This approach not only reduces interpersonal conflicts but also promotes a culture of respect and understanding, where team members feel valued and heard. Implementing the QTIP principle, along with assuming positive intent, creates a robust framework for continuous improvement and effective collaboration, ultimately leading to a more cohesive and productive team.

Effective Communication

While open communication is important, effective communication is essential for ensuring clarity and alignment in the workplace. It involves conveying information clearly and accurately, documenting important interactions, and setting boundaries to manage expectations. Open communication is about fostering a culture of honesty and trust whereas effective communication is about optimizing the delivery and reception of information to achieve the desired outcomes. Both are essential for a productive workplace and managing upward.

> **Clear Communication:** Regular updates and clear communication with managers and team members are vital for maintaining alignment and preventing misunderstandings. This includes providing detailed briefings on project progress, discussing potential issues, and seeking feedback to ensure that everyone is on the same page. Clear communication also involves using precise language and avoiding jargon that could lead to confusion. In some cases, you may have to develop a completely different way of categorizing, naming things, and describing them to be effective in influencing and updating leaders. Making complex things simple is an effective way to approach this. To communicate effectively, focus on simplifying complex ideas. Avoid tailoring your message to how you personally understand or process information—instead, frame it in a way that resonates with your audience and aligns with how they are likely to receive it..

> **Documentation:** Keeping detailed records of interactions, decisions, and communications is an important practice for accountability and reference. Documentation helps track progress, ensures that commitments are met, and provides a written record that can be referred to in case of disputes or misunderstandings. It also

supports transparency and helps in maintaining organizational knowledge, especially in large teams or complex projects. Detailed records are less for your audience (although some might love this detail), but they serve as a resource database that allows you to generate and craft messages, communications, and content that help address many of the manager archetypes.

Setting Boundaries: Defining and communicating availability is crucial for managing work–life balance and preventing burnout. Setting boundaries involves being clear about work hours, response times, and availability for meetings. It helps manage expectations and ensures that professionals can maintain productivity without compromising their well-being. Setting boundaries also fosters mutual respect and understanding among colleagues and managers.

Balancing Crisis With Stability

Balancing the ability to manage crises with the need for stability is crucial for maintaining a productive and positive work environment. This involves stabilizing routine tasks while being prepared to address emergencies effectively.

Be Ready for Disruption: Stabilizing routine tasks and projects ensures that the team can function efficiently even during turbulent times. This involves creating structured processes and clear guidelines that provide a sense of order and predictability. For example, implementing a daily stand-up meeting can help team members stay aligned on routine tasks and quickly address any minor issues before they escalate. At the same time, being prepared to address crises involves having contingency plans and the flexibility to adapt quickly to changing circumstances. Developing a detailed emergency response plan, such as a step-by-step procedure for handling IT outages, ensures that the team can react swiftly and effectively when a crisis occurs. Promoting strategic long-term planning helps in maintaining stability and resilience, as it ensures that the organization is prepared for future challenges.

By integrating these essential coping skills into their professional practices, individuals can build a robust foundation for thriving in the workplace. Anticipation, emotional intelligence, and effective communication form the core of this foundation, supported by self-sufficiency and a balance between crisis management and stability. Together, these skills enable professionals to navigate challenges with confidence, foster positive relationships, and drive continuous growth and success. These horizontal capabilities are not isolated techniques but interwoven strategies that, when practiced consistently, enhance one's ability to manage various manager archetypes effectively. Ultimately, they equip professionals with the resilience and adaptability needed to excel in any work environment, transforming potential obstacles into opportunities for growth.

CHAPTER 11

Building Resilience

When I landed my dream job at Microsoft, it felt like I had reached the pinnacle of my professional life. The sense of accomplishment was immense, but it was quickly overshadowed by a crippling sense of imposter syndrome. Surrounded by some of the brightest minds in the industry, I felt like a small fish trying to swim in an ocean of overwhelming talent. Every day, I was consumed by the fear that I would be exposed as a fraud, that my shortcomings would be discovered, and I would be dismissed from this incredible opportunity.

Despite my anxieties, I poured myself into my work. Driven by the fear of being unmasked, I pushed myself harder than ever before. This relentless drive led to significant achievements. I received overwhelmingly positive feedback from my peers and superiors, accolades that should have bolstered my confidence. I was even double promoted, a testament to my efforts and contributions. Yet, each performance review, no matter how glowing, felt like a mere formality before the inevitable downfall.

I found myself fixated on any hint of criticism, no matter how minor. Every accolade was quickly brushed aside, overshadowed by the relentless pursuit of perfection. I believed that unless I stamped out every perceived weakness, I would never truly unleash my potential. It was a constant battle, focusing on the negatives while ignoring the positives that were right in front of me.

This constant focus on negatives severely impaired my ability to deal with challenging managers. I felt as if I were under the thumb of an out-of-control set of individuals, convinced that no matter how hard I tried, I could only see the negative aspects of their behavior. I languished in the perceived unfairness of the situation, allowing resentment of these managers to color every aspect of my employment experience. The more I achieved, the worse my perception of these individuals' behaviors seemed to poison my job satisfaction. I felt like a hopeless victim of circumstances centered around one or two difficult managers, utterly powerless to change my situation.

This experience underscores a fundamental aspect of human nature: our propensity to look for threats and challenges. Evolution has wired us to prioritize negatives as a survival mechanism. In the modern workplace, this manifests as a focus on weaknesses and potential failures, even in the face of success. We are often our harshest critics, scrutinizing ourselves more intensely than anyone else ever would.

This chapter aims to shift that perspective. By cultivating a positive mental attitude, we can transform how we perceive and handle challenges. A positive outlook not only enhances our professional health, job satisfaction, and career advancement but also equips us with the resilience to deal with difficult manager archetypes. Resilience, built on a foundation of positivity, empowers us to navigate over, under, and around organizational and behavioral obstacles, leading to a more fulfilling and successful career.

In the pages that follow, we'll explore the tangible and intangible benefits of maintaining a positive mental attitude at work. We'll delve into strategies for fostering positivity, from gratitude practices to mindfulness techniques, and examine how these practices can build mental toughness and resourcefulness. Through real-life examples and practical advice, you'll learn how to harness the power of positivity to thrive in any professional environment, even when faced with the most challenging managers.

As for my own situation described previously, through trial and error, I gradually found the inner strength to recognize the detrimental cycle I had trapped myself in. It was with the support of key mentors, relationship guidance, and insightful advice from great managers that I began to see that I had allowed myself to be ensnared in a whirlpool of negativity. These mentors and managers helped me realize that I alone had the power to control my experiences and outlook, as well as my reactions to the challenges I faced. This epiphany was not a quick fix; it required dedication, persistence, and a conscious effort to overcome my negativity-seeking tendencies.

Implementing the right techniques to manage difficult manager archetypes didn't yield immediate results either. I had to be determined, continuously work at it, and consistently guard against slipping back into a downward negative spiral. It became clear that while it's easy to see threats and focus on negativity, striving to find and maintain a positive outlook is a more challenging, yet rewarding, path. I chose to embrace this challenge, taking the high road by seeking out positives and shielding myself from the storm of undesirable and negative behavior.

In this chapter, we will consolidate everything we've learned so far and delve into how to develop a positive mental attitude. We will explore how to protect this mindset as a fundamental part of building innate resilience. By adopting these strategies, you can transform your professional experience, no matter the challenges you face.

Importance of a Positive Mental Attitude

Imagine waking up every day with a mindset tuned to spot opportunities rather than obstacles, to see potential instead of problems. This shift in perspective is what a positive mental attitude offers, and its impact on personal and professional life is profound. Despite the term's seeming imprecision, the benefits of cultivating and safeguarding a positive mental attitude are both tangible and transformative.

In my journey, adopting a positive mental attitude became a cornerstone of my professional development. Initially, I was skeptical about the real impact of such an abstract concept. However, through consistent practice and mindful application, I began to experience significant changes. I noticed that my stress levels decreased, my ability to handle pressure improved, and my interactions with colleagues became more harmonious. This was not just about feeling good; it was about becoming resilient, adaptable, and more effective in my role.

Scientific research supports the benefits of a positive outlook. Studies have shown that a positive mental attitude can lead to better health outcomes, increased job satisfaction, and higher levels of productivity. For instance, a study by the Mayo Clinic highlights that positive thinking helps with stress management and can even improve health by boosting the immune system and increasing lifespan (AllBusiness.com). In the workplace, positivity can enhance creativity and problem-solving abilities, making it easier to navigate complex challenges and develop innovative solutions.

As I began to implement this mindset, the changes were not immediate but gradually became evident. I worked hard to replace my habitual negativity with a focus on the positive aspects of my work and interactions. This shift wasn't easy—it required determination, persistence, and a conscious effort to maintain. Over time, however, the benefits became undeniable. I started to be included in more critical sessions, invited to executive conversations, and seen as a valuable contributor to the organization's success.

My positive attitude began to act as a kind of organizational lubricant, enhancing performance and fluidity within the team. Colleagues and managers alike appreciated how I addressed challenges with a calm and constructive approach. They heralded my positive outlook as an intangible benefit, one that significantly contributed to our collective ability to achieve results. This perception translated into tangible rewards, as my career advancement accelerated. I was given more responsibilities, leadership opportunities, and recognition, all of which were directly linked to the positive energy and resilience I brought to the workplace.

Cultivating and protecting a positive mental attitude is more than just a feel-good mantra; it is a strategic approach to professional and personal growth. By focusing on the positives, you can build resilience, enhance your problem-solving skills, and create a supportive and productive work environment. Embracing this mindset can transform your professional experience, leading to greater job satisfaction, improved health, and accelerated career advancement. The benefits of a positive mental attitude are real and far-reaching, proving that sometimes, the most impactful changes come from within.

Developing a Positive Mental Attitude

In professional settings, altering our perception can significantly enhance our ability to cope with challenging situations and to cultivate a positive mental attitude. By integrating mindfulness, understanding emotional boundaries, and conducting gratitude-based evaluations, we can transform how we perceive and respond to workplace dynamics.

Mindfulness: Recognizing Negative Spirals

One surprising thing I learned is that you may already be in a negative spiral. In many cases, I found that I didn't even realize just how much of a downward, jaded spiral I was in. While in the midst of this pain, if someone came along with some talk about developing a positive mental attitude, I'd quickly invite them to take a long walk off of a short pier. However, recognizing and coming to terms with just how jaded you are, allows you the perspective to determine what your next steps might be.

Mindfulness is a powerful tool for recognizing when we are caught in a negative spiral. It involves being present and fully engaged in the moment, allowing us to observe our thoughts and feelings without judgment. Observing the core impetus behind our professional attitudes and negativity can help us identify whether we are in a negative spiral. Research by Hofmann et al. (2010) demonstrates that mindfulness-based therapy can significantly reduce symptoms of anxiety and depression, making it a valuable tool for managing workplace stress.[*] Often, we don't realize how jaded we have become until we take a step back and examine ourselves. Mindfulness practices, such as meditation or reflective journaling, can illuminate these patterns and provide clarity. Sometimes, skilled therapy is required to help us delve deeper into these issues, but the first step is recognizing the spiral. Of course, there can be clinical or more serious reasons as to why this phenomenon occurs and addressing them with the right mixture of professional and medical guidance is the best thing we can do. In many cases, simple awareness

[*] Hofmann et al., 2010, "The Effect of Mindfulness-Based Therapy on Anxiety and Depression: A Meta-Analytic Review, *Journal of Consulting and Clinical Psychology*, https://psycnet.apa.org/doiLanding?doi=10.1037%2Fa0018555.

alone can begin the road back to positivity. By catching ourselves early, we can implement strategies to shift our mindset and avoid further descent into negativity.

Their Emotions Are Not Your Emotions

One fundamental principle in maintaining a positive mental attitude is understanding that the emotions of others and how they express them, their attitudes and reactions are not contagious and do not have to be internalized. Just because a negative manager behavior has levied undesirable consequences does not mean you need to adopt the same negative emotional state. It's important to give yourself permission to experience feelings of disappointment or melancholy, but also to realize that you don't have to suffer from emotional contagion. Empathize with others and understand their emotions but maintain a healthy separation. This practice helps avoid being sucked into a collective negative spiral. According to Beck (1979), cognitive therapy helps in recognizing and altering distorted thinking patterns, crucial for maintaining emotional boundaries in professional settings.[†] By drawing clear boundaries between your emotional state and that of others, you can maintain your equilibrium and respond more effectively to professional challenges. This separation allows you to support your colleagues and managers without compromising your own mental well-being.

Conduct a Holistic Gratitude-Based Evaluation of Your Professional Journey

Conducting a holistic gratitude-based evaluation of your professional journey can pivot your mindset from a negative to a positive perspective. Instead of asking, "What will I do?" or "What do I have to do?" reframe the question to "What do I get to do next?" This small shift in language is powerfully freeing, granting you control over your responses to challenges, whether situational or managerial. Emmons & McCullough (2003) found that practicing gratitude can significantly enhance mental

---

[†] Beck. *Cognitive Therapy and the Emotional Disorders* (Penguin, 1979).

health and life satisfaction, highlighting the importance of gratitude-based evaluations in professional development.[‡] Reflect on your career, considering where you've been, what you've overcome, and where you'd like to be. Visualize yourself looking back with pride on how you responded to challenges, rather than how you reacted impulsively. This reflective practice builds a foundation for positivity by acknowledging past successes and setting a positive tone for future endeavors. Gratitude enhances resilience, providing a buffer against stress and increasing overall job satisfaction.

By integrating mindfulness to recognize negative spirals, maintaining emotional boundaries, and conducting gratitude-based evaluations, professionals can alter their perceptions and foster a positive mental attitude. These practices not only enhance individual well-being but also contribute to a more productive and harmonious workplace. As you implement these strategies, you'll find yourself more included in sessions, invited to executive conversations, and seen as an organizational asset. Your positive attitude will be recognized as an intangible benefit, ultimately paying dividends in terms of career advancement and job satisfaction.

Note that while the suggestions provided in the chapter are valuable and supported by psychological research, they are not substitutes for professional mental health care when dealing with deeper issues. Integrating these practices can enhance day-to-day resilience and positivity, but seeking professional engagement remains crucial for addressing more serious concerns.

[‡] Emmons and McCullough, 2003, "Counting Blessings Versus Burdens: An Experimental Investigation of Gratitude and Subjective Well-Being in Daily Life," *Journal of Personality and Social Psychology,* https://psycnet.apa.org/doiLanding?doi=10.1037%2F0022-3514.84.2.377.

CHAPTER 12

Growing Your Manager

Imagine being able to not only cope with difficult manager archetypes but actually influence them toward better, more effective behaviors. Welcome to the world of "managing upward." This concept may sound daunting, but it's rooted in empathy and understanding. By mastering these techniques, you can create a more harmonious work environment and enhance your professional relationships. This chapter is a succinct wrap-up of the guidance provided throughout this book, focusing on using empathy-founded techniques to grow your managers beyond their challenging behaviors. Let's explore how you can positively influence managerial and leadership behavior, enhancing team dynamics along the way.

Understanding the Concept of Managing Upward

The concept of managing upward, though it might seem modern, is not new. It has its roots in the management theories of the mid-20th century, evolving from traditional hierarchical structures where subordinates were expected to simply follow orders without question. Managing upward emerged as a strategy to foster more dynamic, interactive, and mutually beneficial relationships between employees and their supervisors. Initially, it focused on aligning one's work and communication styles to better fit the manager's preferences, aiming for smoother operations and better performance reviews.

In recent years, managing upward has evolved significantly, becoming more powerful when mixed with empathy and understanding. Today, it is seen not merely as a set of tactics but as a comprehensive strategy rooted in mutual benefit and emotional intelligence. This modern approach emphasizes the alignment of objectives and incentives, recognizing that understanding the drivers behind a manager's behaviors can significantly enhance professional relationships and workplace efficiency.

Managing upward now includes identifying with your manager through empathy, striving to understand their goals, pressures, and motivations. This emotional identification allows for more effective communication, greater trust, and improved collaboration. By focusing on mutual benefit, employees can create a supportive environment where both parties thrive. This shift toward empathy transforms managing upward from a transactional approach to a relational one, emphasizing the importance of shared success and emotional alignment in achieving organizational goals.

Managing upward is all about influencing your manager in a way that aligns with their goals while also meeting your own needs. It's about understanding their perspective, building trust, and guiding them toward more positive behaviors. Empathy is at the heart of this process, enabling you to see the world through your manager's eyes and respond in a way that fosters mutual respect and cooperation.

Key Techniques for Managing Upward

Active Listening: Active listening is the cornerstone of effective communication and a vital tool in managing upward. It means truly engaging with what your manager is saying, asking clarifying questions, and reflecting on their words. When you practice active listening, you demonstrate that you value their input, which builds trust and opens the door to more meaningful dialogue.

Set Clear Expectations: Setting clear expectations is crucial for preventing misunderstandings and ensuring that everyone is on the same page. Open communication about goals, deadlines, and responsibilities helps align your efforts with your manager's expectations. This clarity not only enhances your productivity but also demonstrates your commitment to shared objectives.

Providing Constructive Feedback: Constructive feedback can be daunting, but it's essential for growth. When giving feedback, focus on specific behaviors and their impact, rather than making it personal. Use "I" statements to express how certain actions affect your work and suggest actionable improvements. This approach shows that you care about mutual success and are invested in creating a better working environment.

Empathy-Focused Strategies to Influence Managers

Building Trust and Rapport: Building trust and rapport with your manager takes time and consistent positive interactions. Trust is earned through reliability, honesty, and openness. By consistently delivering on your promises and communicating transparently, you establish a foundation of trust that makes it easier to influence and guide your manager.

Understanding Managerial Goals and Challenges: Take the time to understand your manager's goals and the challenges they face. This insight allows you to align your efforts with their objectives, making your contributions more valuable. Ask questions about their priorities and pressures and offer solutions that can help alleviate their burdens.

Aligning Your Work With Manager's Objectives:

Aligning your work with your manager's objectives demonstrates that you are a team player committed to mutual success. When your efforts support their goals, you create a win–win situation that enhances your value and fosters a more collaborative relationship.

Generalized Techniques From Previous Chapters

Applying Mindfulness and Positivity: Mindfulness and a positive mental attitude are powerful tools for influencing your manager. By staying present and maintaining a positive outlook, you can navigate workplace challenges with grace and resilience. Mindfulness helps you remain calm and focused, while positivity inspires those around you, including your manager.

Enhancing Communication Skills: Effective communication is about clarity, transparency, and consistency. Ensure that your messages are clear and concise, avoid jargon, and tailor your communication style to your manager's preferences. Regular updates and open dialogues foster a sense of shared purpose and understanding.

Promoting a Collaborative Work Environment: Fostering a collaborative work environment benefits everyone, including your manager. Encourage teamwork, celebrate collective successes, and support your colleagues. A positive, collaborative atmosphere not only improves team dynamics but also sets a precedent for your manager to follow.

Growing Your Manager

Consider the story of an employee who effectively and successfully managed upward by building a strong rapport with their manager. This employee practiced active listening, setting clear expectations, and providing constructive feedback. They aligned their projects with the manager's goals and consistently demonstrated their commitment to the team's success. Over time, the manager began to adopt these positive behaviors, leading to a more harmonious and productive work environment. The manager began to count on this employee as a foundational pillar who understood their goals, desires, and aspirations for the organization, for the team, and their own career objectives. The employee became a strategic adviser in these areas, leading the manager to be increasingly open to suggestions, collaboration, and learning.

In this chapter, we've explored the essential techniques for managing upward and influencing your manager positively. By applying empathy, mindfulness, effective communication, and a collaborative spirit, you can grow your manager and enhance team dynamics. Remember, these strategies not only improve your professional environment but also can pave the way for career advancement.

Putting it all Together

As we draw to a close, it's time to reflect on the journey we've taken through the landscape of managerial challenges and the strategies we've developed to navigate them. My own professional achievements have been shaped by decades of determination, grit, and the invaluable advice of others. It wasn't an easy path, but the lessons learned have been profound. In this concluding chapter, we'll synthesize these insights, address common questions, and provide you with conclusive guidance to turn managerial challenges into opportunities for growth.

Common Questions

Throughout my journey of professional growth and navigating challenging managerial dynamics, I've encountered numerous questions that have shaped my understanding and approach. These questions are not only reflective of my firsthand experiences but also resonate with many professionals facing similar challenges. They are the queries that keep us awake at night, the thoughts we mull over during tough times at work, and the reflections that help us grow. As I continue to progress in my career, these questions remain relevant, offering new insights and perspectives with each passing year. In this section, we'll explore some of the most common questions I've asked and continue to ponder. By addressing these queries, we aim to provide you with practical advice and strategies to help you navigate your own professional journey with greater confidence and clarity.

How Do Bad Managers Stay in Their Jobs for So Long?

It's a question many of us have pondered. Bad managers often remain in their positions due to a combination of factors, including organizational inertia, lack of proper feedback mechanisms, and sometimes their own ability to manage upwards effectively. These managers might excel in some areas, such as meeting targets or managing up, which masks their deficiencies in managing their teams effectively. Organizations may also be slow to recognize or act on managerial issues due to complacency or a focus on short-term results.

Often, the reason bad managers—and other employees who aren't particularly good at their jobs—stay in place is that people around them compensate for their behaviors by simply coping without a formalized feedback channel. This creates an environment where poor performance is tolerated and perpetuated. Addressing these issues takes courage and a willingness to step outside of your comfort zone. Implementing the recommendations in this book will undoubtedly cause discomfort, but it's a positive discomfort known as eustress, which is beneficial and promotes growth, unlike distress, which can be harmful.

What If I Recognize Myself in Some of These Archetypes?

Recognizing yourself in some of the manager archetypes can be unsettling, but it's also an opportunity for growth. Self-awareness is the first step toward improvement. Reflect on the behaviors you exhibit and consider how they affect your team. Seek feedback from peers and subordinates and be open to change. Remember to assume positive intent and the QTIP principles from earlier. Embracing empathy, improving communication skills, and being mindful of your actions can help you transition from a challenging manager to a supportive leader.

I Feel Like I Have No Options Left, What Can I Do?

Feeling trapped in a challenging work environment can be overwhelming. However, there are always options. Start by reassessing your situation and identifying aspects you can control. Engage in open and honest communication with your manager, seeking to understand their perspective while expressing your own needs. If internal resolution seems impossible, consider exploring opportunities within other departments or even outside the organization. Remember, maintaining a positive mental attitude and resilience is crucial during such times.

Wrapping up

Realization: People Don't Quit Jobs, They Quit Leaders

One of the most significant realizations in my career was understanding that people don't quit jobs; they quit leaders. This underscores the immense responsibility that comes with leadership. As we've explored throughout this book, the impact of a manager on their team's morale and productivity cannot be overstated. A positive, empathetic leader can inspire and retain talent, while a negative one can drive even the most dedicated employees away.

Eustress versus Distress

Understanding the difference between eustress (positive stress) and distress (negative stress) is vital for managing your well-being and that of your team. Eustress can motivate and energize you, pushing you to achieve your best. In contrast, distress can lead to burnout and disengagement. By fostering a positive work environment and managing stress effectively, you can turn potential stressors into opportunities for growth and development.

Summarizing Key Takeaways and Encouraging Readers to Apply the Strategies

Throughout this book, we've discussed various strategies for managing difficult managers, from developing empathy and emotional intelligence to enhancing communication and promoting collaboration. These strategies are not just theoretical; they are practical tools that can transform your professional life. I encourage you to apply these techniques, experiment with them, and adapt them to your unique situation. The more you practice, the more natural they will become.

Final Thoughts on Turning Managerial Challenges Into Opportunities for Growth

Every managerial challenge is an opportunity for growth. By approaching these challenges with a positive mental attitude and a willingness to learn, you can not only improve your own professional experience but also contribute to a healthier, more productive workplace. Remember, it's not about putting people in boxes but about understanding behaviors and finding ways to influence and improve them.

Courageous Discussions

Having courageous discussions with your managers and colleagues is essential for fostering a transparent and supportive work environment. These conversations may be uncomfortable, but they are necessary for growth and improvement. Approach them with empathy, clarity, and a focus on mutual benefit. By addressing issues head-on and working collaboratively towards solutions, you can create a more positive and dynamic workplace.

Perspective on My Journey

It took me decades of determination, grit, and learning from the advice of others rather than through pain to reach where I am today. Over the years, I began to notice patterns in managerial behavior, recognizing that many archetypes exhibited the same behaviors across diverse groups. It was easy to put people in boxes, but this approach was neither productive nor positive. I had to stop fighting against empathy and emotional intelligence.

Once I embraced these qualities, I was able to influence and manage upwards effectively. By understanding and empathizing with my managers, imagining what a day behind their desk looked like, I could build rapport and trust. This didn't work every time, but maintaining a positive mental attitude made me an irresistible force for good within the organization. My efforts were recognized, and I found myself included in more critical sessions, invited to executive conversations, and seen as a key contributor to the organization's success.

My journey was not about overcoming challenges alone but about transforming those challenges into opportunities for growth. By adopting the strategies discussed in this book and maintaining a positive, empathetic approach, you too can navigate and thrive in any professional environment. Remember, the goal is to grow together, creating a workplace where everyone can succeed.

Appendixes

The table below summarizes the main characteristics and coping strategies for eight manager archetypes that are discussed in detail in the previous chapters as well as how you can cope with the more challenging aspects of these archetypes' behaviors. Use it as a handy guide to identify and deal with the archetypes you encounter in your professional career. Remember, archetypes are not fixed or rigid; they are dynamic and changing.

Archetype	Brief Description	Coping Strategies Summary
The Surprised	The Deer-in-Headlights Boss: Always caught off guard by issues, even when previously informed.	Anticipate Needs: Keep them informed proactively to avoid surprises. Regular Updates: Schedule frequent check-ins to discuss progress and issues. Empathy: Understand their challenges.
The Emergency Broadcaster	The Chicken Little Boss: Believes every minor issue is a major crisis and panics frequently.	Stay Calm: Don't get swept up in the panic. Prioritize: Focus on what really needs attention. Set Boundaries: Gently remind them of your limits and current priorities.
The Complainer	The Woe-is-Me Boss: Constantly complains about problems without seeking solutions.	Active Listening: Acknowledge their concerns without joining the pity party. Redirect Focus: Shift the conversation to solutions. Stay Positive: Keep the mood upbeat.
The Amnesiac	The Forgetful Leader: Frequently forgets past discussions, decisions, and promises.	Documentation: Keep detailed records of meetings and decisions. Follow-Up: Send summaries and reminders. Patience: Gently remind them of past discussions.
The Firefighter	The Crisis Junkie: Thrives on managing crises, often creating emergencies to feel important.	Prioritize Tasks: Separate urgent from important tasks. Stay Organized: Use tools to manage tasks and deadlines. Set Boundaries: Clarify what constitutes a true emergency.
The Order Taker	The Agreeable Follower: Always agrees with superiors, avoids making independent decisions.	Encourage Initiative: Suggest ideas and alternatives. Provide Support: Help them build confidence to make decisions. Set Clear Expectations: Define roles and responsibilities.

Archetype	Brief Description	Coping Strategies Summary
The Raw Nerve	The Overly Sensitive Boss: Reacts emotionally to feedback and criticism, often taking things personally.	Stay Calm: Avoid triggering their sensitivity. Choose Words Carefully: Use gentle, constructive language. Build Trust: Show empathy and understanding consistently.
The Attack Sub	The Stealthy Saboteur: Engages in undermining behaviors and indirect attacks on colleagues.	Stay Professional: Maintain a calm, professional demeanor
The LIFO (Last in First Out)	The Fickle Manager: Frequently changes priorities, often abandoning tasks or projects halfway through.	**Adaptability**: Be prepared for sudden changes. **Communicate Clearly**: Keep open lines of communication. **Stay Positive**: Focus on the bigger picture and your long-term goals.

References

1. Workforce.com. 2023. "The State of (Mis)Communication." Accessed May 21, 2024. www.workforce.com.

2. 2017. "The Effects of Negative Leadership on Employee Outcomes." *Journal of Business Ethics*. Accessed May 21, 2024. https://link.springer.com/journal/10551.

3. 2018. "Toxic Bosses: The Impact of Negative Leadership on Employee Well-being." *Harvard Business Review*. Accessed May 21, 2024. https://hbr.org.

4. 2016. "The Impact of Cognitive Overload on Managerial Performance." *Journal of Management Studies*. Accessed May 21, 2024. https://onlinelibrary.wiley.com/journal/14676486.

5. 2018. "Crisis Mode: Effects on Long-Term Organizational Stability." *Harvard Business Review*. Accessed May 21, 2024. https://hbr.org.

6. Deloitte Consulting LLP. n.d. "Fixing the Overload Problem at Work." Deloitte Insights. Accessed May 21, 2024. www2.deloitte.com/us/en/insights.

7. Sy, Thomas, Stéphane Côté, and Richard Saavedra. 2005. "The Contagious Leader: Impact of the Leader's Mood on the Mood of Group Members, Group Affective Tone, and Group Processes." *Journal of Applied Psychology* 90(2): 295–305. https://doi.org/10.1037/0021-9010.90.2.295.

8. Hofmann, Stefan G., Alice T. Sawyer, Ashley A. Witt, and Diane Oh. 2010. "The Effect of Mindfulness-Based Therapy on Anxiety and Depression: A Meta-Analytic Review." *Journal of Consulting and Clinical Psychology* 78(2): 169–183. https://doi.org/10.1037/a0018555.

9. Beck, Aaron T. 1979. *Cognitive Therapy and the Emotional Disorders*. NY, New York: Penguin.

10. Emmons, Robert A. and Michael E. McCullough. 2003. "Counting Blessings Versus Burdens: An Experimental Investigation of Gratitude and Subjective Well-Being in Daily Life." *Journal of Personality and Social Psychology* 84(2): 377–389. https://doi.org/10.1037/0022-3514.84.2.377.

About the Author

Eric Charran is a seasoned executive with over 25 years of experience leading diverse teams and driving innovation across multiple industries. His career has been dedicated to fostering collaborative environments and guiding organizations through the complexities of technological advancement.

In various leadership roles, Eric has consistently prioritized the development of his team members and the achievement of strategic goals. His pragmatic approach and commitment to continuous learning have earned him recognition as a trusted and effective leader.

What sets Eric apart is the authenticity of his insights. Each story and interaction detailed in his work is drawn directly from real conversations and situations he had to navigate. Through trial and error, Eric developed a set of productive, mutually beneficial coping skills that not only helped advance his career but also provided invaluable lessons for others. These real-world anecdotes and managerial archetypes offer readers practical advice on managing workplace challenges effectively.

Eric's writing is infused with his passion for positive leadership and adaptability in today's ever-evolving business landscape. His commitment to helping others grow and succeed shines through in every piece of guidance he offers, making this book a must-read for professionals at any stage of their career.

Index

OTHER TITLES IN THE BUSINESS CAREER DEVELOPMENT COLLECTION

Vilma Barr, Consultant, Editors

- *High Impact at Low Decibels* by Mike Schiller
- *Classroom to Workplace* by Lynn Appelbaum
- *Working in Business and Finance* by Joseph Malgesini
- *Make Your Internship Count* by Marti Fischer
- *Sales Excellence* by Eden White
- *How to Think Strategically* by Greg Githens
- *Succeeding as a Young Entrepreneur* by Harvey Morton
- *The Intentional Mindset* by Jane Frankel
- *Still Room for Humans* by Stan Schatt
- *Am I Doing This Right?* by Tony D. Thelen Matthew C. Mitchell Jeffrey A.
- *Telling Your Story, Building Your Brand* by Henry Wong
- *Social Media Is About People* by Cassandra Bailey Dana M. Schmidt
- *Pay Attention!* by Cassandra M. Bailey Dana M. Schmidt
- *Remaining Relevant* by Karen Lawson
- *The Road to Champagne* by Alejandro Colindres Frañó
- *Burn Ladders. Build Bridges* by Alan M. Patterson
- *Decoding Your STEM Career* by Peter J Devenyi

Concise and Applied Business Books

The Collection listed above is one of 30 business subject collections that Business Expert Press has grown to make BEP a premiere publisher of print and digital books. Our concise and applied books are for...

- Professionals and Practitioners
- Faculty who adopt our books for courses
- Librarians who know that BEP's Digital Libraries are a unique way to offer students ebooks to download, not restricted with any digital rights management
- Executive Training Course Leaders
- Business Seminar Organizers

Business Expert Press books are for anyone who needs to dig deeper on business ideas, goals, and solutions to everyday problems. Whether one print book, one ebook, or buying a digital library of 110 ebooks, we remain the affordable and smart way to be business smart. For more information, please visit www.businessexpertpress.com, or contact sales@businessexpertpress.com.